Ministry of Planning
Kurdistan Regional Government

Calculating the Gross Regional Product of the Kurdistan Region—Iraq

Sponsored by the Kurdistan Regional Government

Shmuel Abramzon
Nicholas Burger
Peter Glick
Krishna B. Kumar
Cheryl K. Montemayor
Nelly Mejia
Shanthi Nataraj
Francisco Perez-Arce
Claude Messan Setodji

RAND LABOR AND POPULATION

For more information on this publication, visit www.rand.org/t/rr1405

The authors of this report are listed in alphabetical order.

Library of Congress Cataloging-in-Publication Data
ISBN: 978-0-8330-9263-2

Cover Image: Sulaimani city panorama. By Dyar se via Flicker.

Published by the RAND Corporation, Santa Monica, Calif.

Preface

Comprehensive and reliable statistics are crucial for policy formulation in any region or country. Statistics make it possible to identify the most pressing needs, track progress of policies and initiatives currently in place, and plan future development. Most important, statistics form the foundation for successful policy planning in many areas. The Kurdistan Regional Government (KRG) has been hampered by the lack of such statistics as it charts a course toward peace and prosperity, and invited RAND to assist in designing a policy-relevant data collection system for the Kurdistan Region—Iraq (KRI).

Past RAND efforts were aimed at designing an overall strategy for a policy-relevant data collection system for the KRI and building capacity at the Kurdistan Region Statistics Office (KRSO) through the implementation of a labor force survey. In this report, we describe our efforts to continue building capacity at the KRSO by setting up a system for data collection and analysis to support the annual calculation of the gross regional product (GRP), which we recommended as a critical indicator during the initial phase of our efforts for the KRI. In addition to workshops, RAND provided the KRSO with overall guidance and training, both analytical and hands-on in nature. By being involved in the study, the staff of the KRSO benefited from the process of "learning by doing."

The primary intended audience for this report is KRG policymakers and KRSO staff. As such, the report is intended to serve this audience as (1) a summary of our activities for this project, (2) a presentation of key results from our GRP calculation efforts, and (3) a reference guide that can be used for future GRP calculations. We also aim to make this report accessible to general readers who may be interested in the structure of the KRI economy, in how capacity building for central statistical organizations can be carried out, and in the calculation of GRP.

This research was undertaken within RAND Labor and Population. RAND Labor and Population has built an international reputation for conducting objective, high-quality, empirical research to support and improve policies and organizations around the world. Its work focuses on international development, children and families, demographic behavior, education and training, labor markets, social welfare policy, immigration, financial decisionmaking, and issues related to aging and retirement, all with a common aim of understanding how policy and social and economic forces affect individual decisionmaking and human well-being.

The authors of this report are listed in alphabetic order. Peter Glick and Krishna B. Kumar, senior economists at RAND, are the principal investigators of this study. Dr. Glick may be reached via email at pglick@rand.org or by phone at 703-413-1100 x5426. Dr. Kumar may be reached via email at kumar@rand.org or by phone at 310-393-0411 x7589.

More information about RAND is available on our website: www.rand.org.

Contents

Figures and Tables

Figures

Tables

Summary

Comprehensive and reliable statistics are crucial for policy formulation in any region or country. Statistics make it possible to identify the most pressing needs, track progress of policies and initiatives currently in place, and plan future development. Most important, statistics form the foundation for successful policy planning in many areas. The Kurdistan Regional Government (KRG) has been hampered by the lack of such statistics as it charts a course toward peace and prosperity, so it asked RAND to assist in designing a policy-relevant data collection system for the Kurdistan Region—Iraq (the KRI).

In this report, we discuss our efforts to continue building capacity at the Kurdistan Regional Statistics Office (KRSO) by setting up a system for data collection and analysis to support the annual calculation of the gross regional product (GRP), which we recommended as a critical indicator during the initial phase of our efforts for the KRI. The report presents estimates of the KRI's GRP (excluding natural resources, because of lack of available data) for the year 2012. Three governorates—Erbil, Sulaymaniyah, and Duhok—were covered by the study.

We used existing survey data (for example, in agriculture and manufacturing) or administrative data (for example, in Public Administration and Defense) wherever possible to minimize data collection costs and time. For several sectors (for example, construction and miscellaneous services), no such data were available, and we worked with the KRSO to develop and conduct new surveys to obtain enterprise data on revenues and costs for the value added calculations. The relevant chapters of the report note the data sources and their limitations for the value added calculation for each sector.

We generally use the *production approach* to estimate the contribution of different sectors to GRP. This approach calculates income, or value added, as the value of production or output minus the cost of goods used in production, or intermediate inputs. In addition, we used administrative data from the various KRG ministries and agencies to calculate value added by the public sector. In this case, and for several other sectors, such as the financial sector, the production approach is not possible, and we instead use the *income approach*, in which statistical data are used to sum up the various components that constitute income generated from production: compensation of employees, rent payments, net taxes on production, consumption of fixed capital, and profits (or losses).

We calculate value added by each sector using the relevant and feasible approach for each case, then sum up the sector value added figures to derive the GRP for the entire region. Our calculations exclude the natural resources sector, because of the constantly changing nature of this sector and data considerations. During this process, we continued to build capacity, both through workshops and by carrying out the GRP estimation in collaboration with KRSO staff, with the goal of building capacity through "learning by doing." During this process, we have also consulted with a team of three external advisors to the project, each of whom is an expert on GDP calculation.

We estimate the non-oil GRP of the KRI in 2012 to be 27,381 billion Iraqi dinars (ID), or 23.52 billion U.S. dollars (USD). Table S.1 and Figure S.1 summarize the sector-wide breakdown of value added.

The largest nongovernment sectors in terms of value added to the KRI in 2012 were construction (18.7 percent), wholesale and retail trade (9.1 percent), home ownership and rental (8.6 percent), and miscellaneous services (7.3 percent). The large contribution of construction to value added is consistent with the KRI's rapid economic growth. As elsewhere in the Middle East region, public administration plays a very large role in the economy, accounting for 27.6 percent of value added. It is important to note that, because of the use of the income approach for this sector, value added includes both current operations and internally undertaken investment expenditures.

Table S.1
Value Added, by Sector, in the Kurdistan Region—Iraq

Sector	ISIC Rev. 4 Code	Value Added (ID, billions)	Value Added (USD, billions)	Percentage of Total Value Added
Agriculture	A 01–03	840.1	0.72	3.1
Quarrying	B 05–09	42.5	0.037	0.2
Manufacturing	C 10–33	1,681.5	1.44	6.1
Electricity	D 35	555.9	0.48	2.0
Water	E 36–39	Included in public administration		
Construction	F 41–43	5,130.8	4.41	18.7
Wholesale and retail trade	G 45–47	2,499	2.15	9.1
Transportation and storage	H 49–53	1,752.9	1.51	6.4
Accommodation and food service	I 55–56	854.5	0.73	3.1
Information and communications (large firms)	J 58–63	1,844.3	1.58	6.7
Banking, insurance, money exchanges	K 64–66	305.3	0.26	1.1
Miscellaneous services	L, M, N, P, Q, R, S	1,999.6	1.72	7.3
Public administration	O 84	7,577.3	6.51	27.6
Home ownership and rental		2,355	2.02	8.6
Total value added		27,439	23.57	100.0
Plus: product taxes		0.223	0.0002	
Less: FISIM		58.4	0.0502	
Gross regional product		27,381	23.52	

NOTES: The codes in the second column are from United Nations, Department of Economic and Social Affairs, Statistics Division, *International Standard Classification of Economic Activities Revision 4*, 2008c. FISIM = financial intermediation services indirectly measured (discussed in Chapter Eleven).

Figure S.1
Value Added, by Sector, in the Kurdistan Region—Iraq

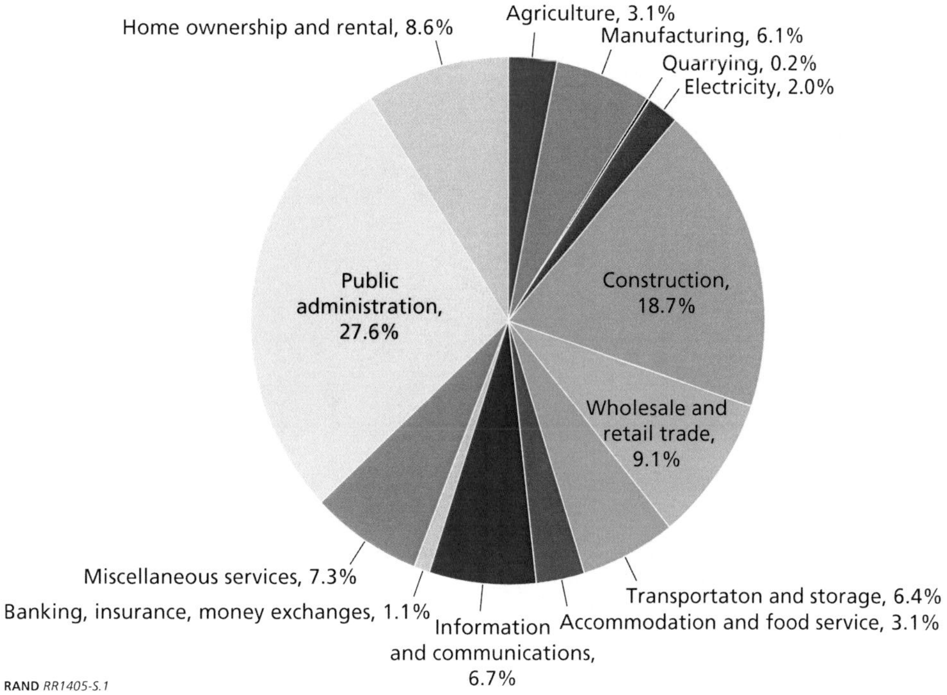

RAND *RR1405-S.1*

Also consistent with the region overall, the KRI's share of value added in agriculture is low (3.1 percent). This is the same as that reported by Jordan in 2012 (3.1 percent) and somewhat lower than that of Lebanon 6.1 percent) and Turkey (8.8 percent). Manufacturing contributed 6.1 percent of value added. This share is substantially lower than that reported by other countries in the region (19 percent for Jordan, 9 percent for Lebanon, 17 percent for Turkey), suggesting that there is room for expansion of this sector as a source of future growth in the KRI.[1]

This report is the first comprehensive attempt to calculate GRP for the KRI. Due to constraints on data availability (and the fact that carrying out new comprehensive, economy-wide data collection was well beyond the scope of the project), we faced two main challenges in value added calculations for some sectors. First, the value added estimates in this report rely heavily on the most recent listing of firms, which was done in 2009. Given the recent, rapid growth in the region, it is highly likely that the number of firms in various sectors of the economy grew between 2009 and 2012, which might cause us to underestimate value added. Second, there are several sectors in which a few firms contribute a large share of value added. Examples include banking, telecommunications, and publishing. We attempted to capture as many of these large firms as possible through interviews and publicly available information, but we were unable to obtain complete information on all of these large firms.

In the future, estimates of GRP would be improved by putting into place a set of streamlined and standardized procedures to gather the required information on value added from *all* sectors. The backbone of these procedures would be the implementation of an enterprise

[1] Data for Jordan, Lebanon, and Turkey are from World Bank (2015).

census. The best practice is to conduct an enterprise census every few years (the "benchmark" years). During interim years, it is advisable to count and gather limited information on revenues and employment from all large and medium firms, to ensure that the firms that account for the largest share of value added are fully represented. A subset of firms may also be more fully surveyed in interim years. Putting into place such a system will also make it easier to update GRP for the KRI on an annual and systematic basis.

Acknowledgments

We are grateful to the Kurdistan Regional Government (KRG) for supporting this research. Although we have benefited immensely from the feedback and support we have received from numerous KRG officials, we are particularly indebted to His Excellency Dr. Ali Sindi, Minister of Planning; Mr. Serwan Mohamed, Director of the Kurdistan Regional Statistics Office (KRSO); Mr. Zagros Fatah, General Director, Ministry of Planning; and Dr. Jamal Ameen, Senior Advisor, Ministry of Planning.

We also want to acknowledge the talented and dedicated staff of the KRSO, who have worked so hard to make the first comprehensive effort to calculate the gross regional product (GRP) of the Kurdistan Region—Iraq a success. In particular, we would like to thank Mr. Morad Zaynal Ahmad, Mr. Abdulkhaliq Mohamad Mostafa, Mr. Mohammad Sabir Omar, Mr. Dlawar Jalil Ahmad, Ms. Hadar, Ms. Tara Abdulghani Khalil, Ms. Basima Hanna Sabo, Ms. Fatma Omer Ali, Mr. Bashdar Ayub Kareem, Mr. Soran Habib, and Mr. Soran Franci.

We are also grateful for the efforts of Ms. Zheen Sanan Emin Almukhtar, Mr. Hersh Ali Hasan, and Mr. Awat Mustafa.

We are grateful to an external panel of experts in national income accounting, including Mr. Peter Gardiner, Mr. Roger Jullion, and Mr. Viet Vu Quang, for their advice on methodological approaches to the GRP calculations. We also thank two anonymous referees for their valuable comments.

At RAND, we benefited from the guidance and support of the Labor and Population Unit. We are also grateful to Ms. Robin Meili, director of International Programs, who coordinated the suite of RAND studies.

CHAPTER ONE

Introduction

Project Background and Purpose

Comprehensive and reliable statistics are crucial for policy formulation in any region or country. Statistics make it possible to identify the most pressing needs, track progress of policies and initiatives currently in place, and plan future development. Most important, statistics form the foundation for successful policy planning in many areas. The Kurdistan Regional Government (KRG) has been hampered by the lack of such statistics as it charts a course toward peace and prosperity, so it invited RAND to assist in designing a policy-relevant data collection system for the Kurdistan Region—Iraq (the KRI) (Abramzon et al., 2014; Anthony et al., 2015).

Past RAND efforts were aimed at designing an overall strategy for a policy-relevant data collection system for the KRI, and building capacity at the Kurdistan Region Statistics Office (KRSO) through the implementation of a labor force survey. In this report, we summarize our efforts to continue building capacity at the KRSO by setting up a system for data collection and analysis to support the annual calculation of the gross regional product (GRP), which we recommended as a critical indicator during the initial phase of our efforts for the KRI. The report presents estimates of the KRI's GRP (excluding natural resources) for the year 2012. Three governorates—Erbil, Sulaymaniyah, and Duhok—were covered by the study. Our calculations exclude the natural resources sector because of the lack of availability of data; in Chapter Fifteen, we present recommendations on the type of data that KRG will need to compile to calculate value added from this sector.

Approach

Estimation of GRP is conceptually equivalent to the estimation of gross domestic product (GDP) of a region. After engaging in cross-country benchmarking, and in line with most international practices, we chose to estimate the GRP of the KRI using the production approach. The production approach estimates GDP by aggregating the gross value added by firms in the economy, where gross value added is the value of output net of costs of materials and services used in production (that is, net of the costs of intermediate goods). The value of intermediate goods is netted out to avoid double counting; the intermediate goods are counted as value added for *their* producers. Figure 1.1 illustrates the gross value added concept.

One of the main advantages of the production approach for calculating regional GDP is that it eliminates the need for data on inter-regional flows, which are typically difficult to

Figure 1.1
Illustration of the Gross Value Added Concept

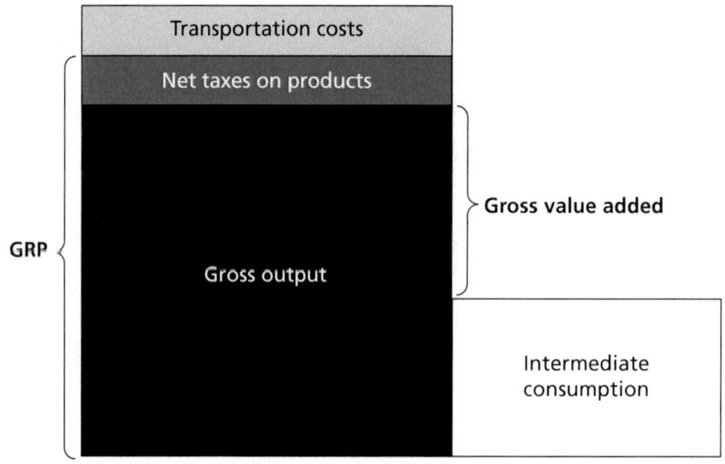

RAND *RR1405-1.1*

obtain. In principle, estimating GRP by the other main approaches, the *income approach* or the *expenditure approach*, will yield the same estimate of regional GDP.

The production approach requires data on two main aggregates: (1) the output produced by regional residents and (2) intermediate consumption by them. Gross value added is then calculated by subtracting the latter from the former. In calculating GRP, we sum up all the gross value added across the region and, as necessary, also add net taxes (taxes minus subsidies) that were not included in the regional output data.

The next paragraphs will touch on the main conceptual issues that arise when calculating GRP.[1]

Output

It is common to collect output data valued at the *basic price* of a good or service. Basic price measures the amount receivable by the producer for one unit of the good or service, *without* including taxes or subsidies on products (such as sales or value added taxes). The product taxes and subsidies are later added back in for the region as a whole. Basic prices *do* include taxes and subsidies on *production*, such as payroll taxes. However, our discussions with staff at the KRSO and in the Ministry of Finance indicate that the KRI does not impose product taxes (value added taxes, sales taxes, or any other taxes that vary with the amount of production), but only production taxes. Thus, we take the taxes reported by firms to be production taxes, and we do not exclude them when calculating output.

The value of output excludes transport costs paid separately by the purchaser to a third party. If the sales value of the product includes transport costs, then the full value of the product and the related transport services are considered to be part of the producer's output. If, instead, the producer paid a third party for transport, then the transport costs are part of the producer's intermediate consumption. In this case, the revenue from the transport service is reflected in the output of the transportation service provider.

[1] Our summary is based on Vu Quang (2009, 2010).

Intermediate Consumption

Intermediate consumption is defined as the cost of all goods and services used up in the production of the output during the accounting period. This includes, generally speaking, all the material and service costs for producing the goods and services. It does not include labor costs, gross interest charges (excluding financial intermediation services indirectly measured, FISIM, which we discuss in Chapter Eleven), capital costs, production taxes, or consumption of capital. Intermediate consumption is typically reported at purchasers' prices—that is, market prices less deductible (such as value added) taxes. Since the KRI does not have a value added tax, we calculate intermediate consumption using the prices reported by firms, which we take to be purchasers' prices.

Using Income Instead of Value Added in Production

As explained, subtracting intermediate consumption from output equals gross value added. But in some cases it is difficult to obtain accurate data on either output or intermediate consumption. This is true, for example, for the Public Administration and Financial sectors. In these cases, we instead use the *income approach*, in which statistical data are used to sum up the various components that constitute income generated from production: compensation of employees, rent payments, net taxes on production, consumption of fixed capital, and profits (or losses).

We calculate value added sector by sector using the relevant approach, then sum up the sector value added figures to get the GRP for the entire region. During this process, we continued to build capacity, both through workshops (as discussed below) and by carrying out the GRP estimation in conjunction with KRSO staff, with the goal of building capacity through "learning by doing." During this process, we also consulted with a team of three external advisors to the project, each of whom is an expert on GDP calculation.

While this broadly describes our approach to calculating GRP, we encountered different challenges in calculating the value added for each sector, necessitating assumptions that we document in the following chapters.

We used existing survey data (for example, in agriculture and industries) or administrative data (for example, in public administration) to minimize costs and time. For several sectors (for example, construction and miscellaneous services), no such data were available, and we worked with the KRSO to conduct new surveys and interviews to collect enterprise data on revenues and costs for the value added calculation. One limitation of this approach is that, for certain sectors, the available data are from either somewhat before or after 2012.[2] The relevant chapters of the report note the specific limitations associated with the value added calculation for each sector. In addition, we used administrative data from the various KRG ministries and agencies to calculate value added by the public sector.

A note about our overall approach is in order. This study is the first comprehensive attempt to calculate GRP for the KRI. Because of constraints on data availability (and the fact that carrying out new comprehensive, economy-wide data collection was well beyond the scope of the

---

[2] All new survey data collection was conducted in 2014 and was completed before the large-scale fighting with the Islamic State and the heavy influx into the KRI of internally displaced persons from elsewhere in Iraq. Disruption from these factors therefore did not affect the survey fieldwork or economic activities recorded in the surveys. However, political challenges were ongoing during the time and likely had some dampening impact on overall economic activity, and may have resulted in recorded activity and revenues below normal levels.

project), we faced various challenges for each sector that might have caused us to underestimate or overestimate value added. In each chapter, we document the specific challenges associated with value added calculations for the sector being discussed. In the concluding chapter, we make some overall recommendations on how GRP for the KRI can be calculated in a more systematic and regular fashion in the future.

Capacity Building

During this project, as in the previous phase, we carried out extensive activities to build capacity at the KRSO. This was done both through workshops and by carrying out the GRP estimation in conjunction with KRSO staff, with the goal of building capacity through "learning by doing." Details of the workshops (all held at the KRSO's offices in Erbil) follow.

Dissemination Workshop

The first workshop, which took place during August and September 2013, consisted of specialized training of the KRSO's new Dissemination Group. This group, currently consisting of five staff members, is responsible for taking reports and other work by various departments of the KRSO (including the GRP estimation) and preparing them for wider dissemination through press releases and other formats on the KRSO website and in hard-copy form. The group had already received training from the United Nations Population Fund. Several other KRSO staff members also attended one or more sessions.

The RAND workshop sessions were developed to complement the training already received and to engage the staff in exercises. The sessions were conducted over the course of three closely timed visits by members of the RAND team. This spacing of sessions facilitated carrying out exercises between sessions.

The following topics were covered:

- purpose of dissemination of national and regional statistics
- ways to identify key audiences
- ways to target information effectively to different audiences
- how to develop effective press releases and policy briefs
- general guidance on written documents
- use of visual tools in written documents
- general guidance on presentations
- quality assurance in dissemination
- modes of dissemination.

GRP Workshop

The second workshop was led by RAND in the second week of December 2013, over the course of two days. In this workshop, the RAND team provided an overview of the various methods of GRP measurement, then focused on specific methods needed to estimate GRP via the production approach. The following topics were covered:

- concepts and definitions
- measurement of gross output in basic prices

- measurement of intermediate consumption at purchasers' prices
- treatment of taxes, subsidies, and transportation costs
- selective use of the income approach for certain sectors
- estimation of value added and GRP
- treatment of cross-regional firms
- inflation, price indices and real GRP
- data sources for GRP calculation.

The RAND team also illustrated the principles discussed by walking through preliminary value added calculations from the agricultural, manufacturing, financial services, electricity, and construction sectors. The presentation emphasized data sources, challenges faced in estimating value added, and methods for addressing these challenges.

In March 2014, the RAND team followed up on initial GRP training by reviewing key aspects of GRP estimation and presenting methods, data sources, and preliminary results from a variety of sectors.

Survey Workshop

A two-day workshop led by RAND was held at the KRSO in the first week of February 2014 to review the drafts of the survey questionnaires for construction, transportation/storage, and other services and to discuss sampling procedures and the uses of the data to be gathered. In addition to KRSO staff from the central office, two senior survey staff persons from each of the three governorate offices attended. The discussion in the workshop led to adjustment in the questionnaires and helped the planning for the fieldwork.

Organization of This Report

In the rest of this report, we provide our estimates of value added by sector, classified by major International Standard Industrial Classification of All Economic Activities (ISIC) Revision 4 codes (United Nations, Department of Economic and Social Affairs, Statistics Division, 2008c):[3]

- Chapter Two: Agriculture (A)
- Chapter Three: Quarrying (B)
- Chapter Four: Manufacturing (C)
- Chapter Five: Electricity (D)
- Chapter Six: Construction (F)
- Chapter Seven: Wholesale and Retail Trade (G)
- Chapter Eight: Transportation and Storage (H)
- Chapter Nine: Accommodation and Food Service (I)
- Chapter Ten: Information and Communications (J)
- Chapter Eleven: Banking, Insurance and Money Exchanges (K)
- Chapter Twelve: Miscellaneous Services (L, M, N, P, Q, R, S)

---

[3] We do not provide a separate value added estimate for Water Supply, Sewerage, Waste Management, and Remediation (Section E) activities, as these are included in Section O (Public Administration and Defense).

- Chapter Thirteen: Public Administration and Defense (O)
- Chapter Fourteen: Households (T).

We conclude in Chapter Fifteen with a summary of our estimates and with recommendations for future practice in collecting data for and estimating the GRP of the KRG, including the natural resource sector, which is not part of the current calculation. Appendixes A through E provide further details for the agriculture, manufacturing, electricity, trade, and banking/insurance/money exchange sectors, respectively. Appendix F presents the sampling methods and describes the questionnaires used for the new surveys.

In a separate online document, Appendix G presents the questionnaires for the "Other Services" and construction surveys, and Appendix H provides the presentations given during the capacity-building workshops.

CHAPTER TWO

Agriculture

This chapter presents estimates for value added from the agricultural sector, based on the agricultural census and a subsequent survey conducted by the KRSO in 2011–2012.

Methods

The Ministry of Agriculture (MoA) and the KRSO conducted agriculture census listings, at the level of farmers within villages, subdistricts, districts, or governorates, during the winter of 2011 and summer of 2012. These census listings registered all farmers and their planted areas by type of crop within the villages visited. This listing is the most reliable source of data on land under cultivation and was used as the sampling frame to conduct agricultural surveys.

All data were sampled, collected, and processed by the MoA and the KRSO. We received reports on agricultural production, farmer-level listings from the census, and survey data. We combined data from the census listing and the surveys to estimate the production and value added at the district and governorate levels. We also compared our estimates of production with those provided in KRSO reports.

The surveys were fielded between November 2011 and May 2012. The agriculture census was used to draw the samples. The strategy used by the KRSO was to randomly select 10 percent of the villages in a subdistrict, and two farmers in each village, based on the census listing. Information collected included yield, prices, expenses, and area under cultivation for each type of crop. Table 2.1 presents the five crops that were registered for winter and the 21 crops

Table 2.1
Main Crops, by Season

		Winter		
Wheat	Barley	Chickpeas	Lentils	Vegetables
		Summer		
Rice	Tomatoes	Beans	Fsteqa arabi	Armenian cucumbers
Sunflowers	Okra	Squash	Green peppers	
Sesame	Eggplant	Watermelon	Cotton	
Grass peas	Cucumbers	Potatoes	Onions	
Corn	String Beans	Melons	Tobacco	

SOURCE: 2011/2012 farm-level agriculture survey.

that were registered for summer. These 26 types of crops are the main agricultural products cultivated in the KRI.

Table 2.2 presents the numbers of villages and farmers in the survey and census. In the census, 19 percent of farmers were from the Duhok governorate, 24 percent from Erbil, and 57 percent from Sulaymaniyah. The surveys contained a higher percentage of farmers from Duhok and a lower percentage from Sulaymaniyah.

For each crop and each governorate, we estimated gross output by multiplying the total production in kilograms times the corresponding price per kilogram. Summer prices were obtained from the KRSO. Winter price data were not directly available, so we used the closest available price data from the KRSO's Consumer Price Index (CPI) files. We calculated intermediate consumption as the total costs for the following items, which were reported for the total planted area:

- plowing
- seeds
- watering
- weed control
- composting
- pesticide
- harvesting
- other expenses
- transportation.

Table 2.2
Number of Farmers Surveyed, by Season, 2011/2012

Season	Governorate	Data	Villages	Farmers
Winter	Duhok	Census listing	968	13,648
		Survey	104	157
	Erbil	Census listing	984	19,962
		Survey	108	164
	Sulaymaniyah	Census listing	2,483	48,681
		Survey	453	528
Summer	Duhok	Census listing	598	6,566
		Survey	598	1,527
	Erbil	Census listing	510	6,046
		Survey	510	1,125
	Sulaymaniyah	Census listing	1,092	12,004
		Survey	942	1,285

SOURCE: Authors' calculations based on the 2011/2012 farm-level agriculture survey and the 2011/2012 agriculture census listings.

Results

Table 2.3 presents value added estimates by season for each governorate, which were obtained by subtracting intermediate consumption from gross output. Appendix A provides a more detailed breakdown by district, governorate, and season. The value added by agriculture for the period 2011/2012 was 840.1 billion Iraqi dinars (ID), or 721.7 million U.S. dollars (USD).[1]

Discussion

We encountered several challenges in estimating value added from agriculture, which are discussed in more detail in Appendix A but which we summarize here, along with our strategies for addressing them:

- Inflating survey values based on the reported sampling strategy led to a large overestimate of the total amount of land under cultivation when compared with the totals obtained directly from the census. Therefore, we instead inflated yields from the survey based on the ratio of land under cultivation reported in the survey and the total amount of land under cultivation reported in the census, by district. In this way, our totals correspond to those for the census, which we assume are accurate.
- In some cases, the census reported that specific crops were planted in certain districts, but survey data were not available for those crops in those districts. To address this issue, we imputed yield per donum in the planted areas indicated in the census where survey data were apparently missing, based on the average yield of the same type of crop at the lowest level of aggregation available.
- As mentioned above, winter crop prices were not available. Therefore, we applied relevant prices gathered by the KRSO for calculating the CPI.[2]

As a check on the data, we also benchmarked our estimates for agricultural yield and value added against several countries in the region, including Iraq overall. The average yield per hectare in the KRI is above the yield for all of Iraq for most major crops (Figure 2.1). The

Table 2.3
Value Added, by Agricultural Sector (ID, billions)

Component	Erbil	Sulaymaniyah	Duhok
(1) Gross output	390.4	476.2	364.9
(2) Intermediate consumption	145.5	138.8	107.2
(3) Gross value added (1– 2)	244.9	337.5	257.7
Overall total	840.1		

[1] All ID values were converted to USD by applying the "buy" rate of 1,164 ID/USD as reported by the Central Bank of Iraq for 2012 (Central Bank of Iraq, no date).

[2] Prices for "Hawler center," the capital city's center, in January 2012, were used from the CPI files. Since the reliability of the price data collected from the various districts seemed uncertain, we chose this populous district for our calculations. The KRSO is in the process of reevaluating the procedures for calculating the CPI, and more reliable and verifiable price data are likely to be available for future GRP calculations.

Figure 2.1
Yield of Major Crops for Neighboring Countries

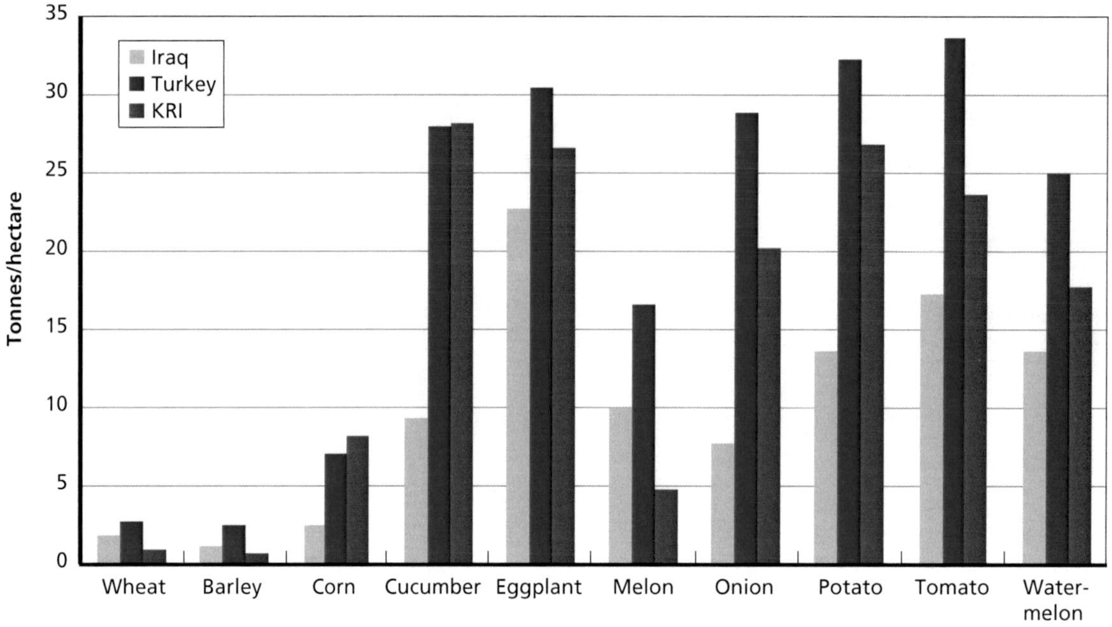

SOURCE: Food and Agriculture Organization of the United Nations, FAOSTAT, 2013.
RAND *RR1405-2.1*

KRI's yield per hectare is similar to Turkey's yield for cucumbers and eggplant and is below Turkey's yield for other major crops. The value added for crops in the KRI amounted to 840.4 billion ID (722 million USD), equivalent to 3.1 percent of GRP. This figure is similar to the value added by crops in Jordan (see Table 2.4).[3]

Table 2.4
Value Added of Crops as Percentage of GDP/GRP

Country	Total GDP/GRP (billion USD)	Crop Value Added (billion USD)	Crops as % of GDP/GRP
Jordan	28.8	808	2.8
KRI	23.6	722	3.1

SOURCES for Jordan data: The World Bank, "GDP at Market Prices (current US$)," 2016; Food and Agriculture Organization of the United Nations, 2013.

Based on this benchmarking exercise, the estimated value added by agriculture appears to be reasonable.

[3] The data presented for Jordan in Table 2.4 cover only the value of crops. If the full value of agriculture (which includes forestry, hunting, fishing, crop production, and livestock production) is included, the share of agriculture in Jordan's value added is 3.1 percent.

CHAPTER THREE

Quarrying

This chapter presents estimates for value added from the quarrying sector, based on a report summarizing a survey conducted by the KRSO and the Central Statistical Organisation (CSO) in 2009 (CSO, 2010). As noted in Chapter One, these estimates do not include mining or other natural resources.

Methods

The report indicated that there were 251 quarries employing 2,129 workers. Table 3.1 shows the reported numbers of quarries and workers in each governorate.

For gross output, we summed the values provided for commodity and noncommodity production. Commodity production accounted for nearly all of the value of total production; noncommodity production was reported only in Erbil and included rent received for buildings, as well as transport services provided to third parties. For intermediate consumption, we used the values of supplies used in production; these included fuels, tools, and power, as well as other commodity and service inputs.

Results

Table 3.2 presents estimates of value added for quarrying, which we obtained by subtracting intermediate consumption from gross output. Value added by quarrying is estimated to have been 42.5 billion ID in 2012 (36.6 million USD).

Table 3.1
Numbers of Quarries and Workers, 2009

Governorate	Quarries	Workers
Erbil	84	549
Sulaymaniyah	70	698
Duhok	97	882
Region total	251	2,129

SOURCE: KRSO/CSO survey results, mining and quarrying for private sector, 2009.

Table 3.2
Value Added by the Quarrying Sector (ID, billions)

Component	Erbil	Sulaymaniyah	Duhok
(1) Gross output	23.7	28.4	19.2
(2) Intermediate consumption	10.0	13.7	5.2
(3) Gross value added (1 – 2)	13.7	14.7	14.1
Overall total	42.5		

Discussion

Our estimates for value added in the quarrying sector are based on 2009 data. Given the rapid pace of growth in the KRI between 2009 and 2012, it is likely that the quarrying sector also grew during this time period. Our estimates are thus likely to underestimate value added by this sector in 2012.

CHAPTER FOUR

Manufacturing

This chapter presents estimates for value added from the manufacturing sector, based on a 2011 survey conducted by the KRSO and the CSO.

Methods

The CSO used the 2009 census to identify large, medium, and small manufacturing firms for a survey across Iraq. Firms in the KRI were surveyed by the KRSO, and survey data were analyzed by the CSO. All large firms (those with 30 or more workers) and all medium firms (those with 10–29 workers) were included in the survey; for the much more numerous small firms (those with 1–9 workers), a random sample was taken, as discussed in more detail below (CSO, 2012c). Initial discussions with KRSO staff suggested that all establishments with more than 100 million ID in capital, regardless of employment size, may have been included in the census of large firms. However, a CSO report indicates that the fixed asset criterion was later dropped (CSO, 2012a).

Our review of CSO reports and data files indicates that the surveys covered major manufacturing industries. These surveys classified enterprises according to the ISIC Revision 3 codes at the four-digit level. The manufacturing sector includes 23 broad industry classifications (15–37). We note that the 2009 census frame appears to use ISIC Revision 4 codes, and it is unclear at what point and why the transition was made to the earlier ISIC Revision 3 codes. However, for our purposes and given the relatively broad categories we use for the value added analysis, there was no ambiguity in coding.

Large and Medium Firms

We received firm-level survey data for medium and large firms and calculated gross value added as gross output minus intermediate consumption following UN guidance (United Nations, Department of Economic and Social Affairs, Statistics Division, 2008b), as follows:

Gross output =
Value of shipments/turnover/sales of goods or services produced by the establishment
+ Value of shipments/turnover/sales of all goods and services purchased for resale in the same condition as received
– Purchases of goods and services for resale in the same condition as received
+ Receipts for industrial work done or industrial services rendered to others
+ Other revenues

+ Value of own-account fixed assets
+ Change in work-in-progress
+ Change in inventories of finished goods
– Change in inventories of goods purchased for resale in the same condition as received

Intermediate consumption =
Cost of raw materials and supplies except gas, fuels, and electricity
+ Cost of gas, fuels, and electricity purchased
+ Cost of water and sewerage services
+ Purchases of services except rental
+ Rental payments
– Changes in inventories of materials, fuels, and supplies

We compared our results to those reported by the CSO in its *Report on Private Sector Large Industrial Firms in the Kurdistan Region 2011* (2012a) and *Report on Private Sector Medium Industrial Firms in the Kurdistan Region 2011* (2012b). We were able to verify that the reported numbers were close to what we calculated based on the firm-level data.

Small Firms

We also received data from the CSO from the small firm survey (CSO, 2012c). The CSO report notes that the 2009 census frame was updated by visiting firms to remove those that were closed, had changed activities, or were performing non-industrial activities, leaving a total of 14,772 firms. The firms were divided into 1,080 strata representing 72 activities and 15 governorates. To ensure representation of all activities, up to five firms in each activity were sampled, resulting in a sample of 357 firms. Next, a single-phase stratified random approach was used to sample the remaining firms. For this second phase, 227 firms were sampled, with probability of sampling in each stratum proportional to variation in firm employment. The total sample size was therefore 584 firms.

Unfortunately, based on our correspondence with the CSO and on the information they provided regarding the numbers of sampled firms in each industry, the data file did not appear to be complete, as the sample received was of only 400 firms. We were unable to reconcile the estimated populations of firms and workers from the data file with the estimated populations reported by the CSO. Therefore, for small firms, we relied on aggregate, reported values of production and supplies directly from the CSO's *Report on Private Sector Small Industrial Firms in the Kurdistan Region 2011* (2012c).

Results

Table 4.1 shows the estimated number of firms and workers in each broad industry classification by firm size. Small firms account for 75 percent of employment in this sector. The four largest industries in terms of total employment are food, fabricated metals, nonmetal mineral products, and textiles.

Table 4.2 presents value added estimates, which were obtained by subtracting intermediate consumption from gross output. Value added by manufacturing is estimated to be 1.681 trillion ID (1.44 billion USD). The relatively low values of gross output and value added

Table 4.1
Estimated Numbers of Firms and Workers in the Manufacturing Sector, 2011

ISIC Revision 3 Code	Industry	Large		Medium		Small	
		Firms	Workers	Firms	Workers	Firms	Workers
15	Food	22	1,529	46	697	1,860	8,489
17	Textiles	3	259	2	39	54	118
18	Wearing apparel					3,463	5,268
19	Leather			1	7		
20	Wood			2	26	890	2,493
21	Paper	1	30	1	17		
22	Printing	4	350	4	64	411	1,180
23	Coke, petroleum and nuclear fuel	2	70	4	55		
24	Rubber	3	295	3	38		
25	Products made of oil and coal	4	227	2	34	358	1,581
26	Nonmetal mineral products	33	3,000	149	1,881	473	3,178
27	Basic metals	4	1,352	1	26		
28	Fabricated metal products	6	346	13	204	3,035	8,512
29	Machinery	1	114	3	36		
31	Electrical machinery	3	397	1	11		
36	Miscellaneous	3	252	4	82	940	2,363
	Region total	89	8,221	236	3,217	11,484	33,182

SOURCE: Large and medium firm counts are based on authors' calculations from the firm-level datasets. Small firm counts are based on CSO (2012c).

Table 4.2
Value Added by Manufacturing Sector (ID, billions)

Component	Erbil	Sulaymaniyah	Duhok
(1) Gross output	1,204.0	1,890.4	223.3
(2) Intermediate consumption	570.2	916.4	149.5
(3) Gross value added (1 – 2)	633.8	974.0	73.7
Overall total	1,681.5		

for Duhok reflect the smaller number of firms in this governorate, as well as a different industry/firm size mix. For example, unlike in the other two governorates, there were no medium or large firms in the machinery or electrical machinery industries in Duhok. Appendix B presents more details on methodology and estimates by ISIC code.

Discussion

The key challenge associated with manufacturing sector data (as with a few other sectors) is that the sampling frame was based on the 2009 census. Although the CSO reports noted that the frame was updated to drop closed firms, it is not clear whether new firms—those started after 2009—were included. In addition, it is likely that the number of manufacturing firms has risen since 2009, given overall growth in the KRI. Finally, the CSO survey was conducted in 2011. Thus, it is likely that the estimated value added understates value added by manufacturing in 2012 to some extent.

CHAPTER FIVE

Electricity

This chapter presents estimates for value added from the electricity sector based on data and information from a variety of sources.

According to the information provided by the KRSO, electricity in the KRI is generated by a small number of large electricity generators (including those owned by Mas-Jordan) and a larger number of small generators that operate at the local level. Some electricity is imported from abroad or from other regions of Iraq. Transmission and distribution of the electricity generated by large generators and of imported electricity is conducted by the Ministry of Electricity (MoE).

We therefore calculated value added of the KRI's electricity sector by estimating value added of (1) distribution by the MoE, (2) large generators, and (3) small private generators.[1]

Methods

Distribution by the Ministry of Electricity

We received data on revenues and expenditures for the MoE for 2012. Since the output data seemed to exclude some sources (specifically, regarding payments from the central government), we chose to estimate value added using the income approach, by summing up relevant government expenditures on labor and capital. Based on our discussions with KRSO staff, we included expenditures labeled as "staff expenses," "social benefits," "subsidies" and "other expenses" (which are related to staff benefits), and "expenditures on non-financial assets," which are essentially consumable capital. We treated expenditures entered as "goods and services" as intermediate consumption and hence excluded them.

Large Generators

We received data on the value of electricity purchased by the MoE from seven large generators in the KRI. These data include actual purchases in 2012 as well as committed purchase values. Only actual purchases are included in our estimates of generators' output.

We were unable to obtain information about intermediate consumption or expenditures for these generators. Thus, we investigated reported value-added-to-output ratios from other countries as a means of imputing value added for the KRI from our output data alone. We were unable to identify reliable estimates for countries in the Middle East and North Africa

[1] There is no need to calculate value added for generation by non-KRI-based electricity providers, since this is not part of the KRI's GRP. We assume that the value associated with distribution of the imported electricity, which is part of the KRI's GRP, was included in the MoE's reports.

region; however, we found estimates for several countries in Europe. Based on an average of the European examples, we use a ratio of 40 percent value-added-to-output for large generators in the KRI.[2]

Small Private Generators

According to information provided by the KRSO, all households in the KRI purchase some electricity from small private generators, even if they are also connected to the national grid. Payment for this electricity is fixed based on the electric current chosen (in amperes). The price per ampere is on average 4,250 ID per month,[3] or 51,000 ID per year. According to the KRSO, most households pay for a 4-ampere connection. Given an estimated 894,228 households in the KRI,[4] the total output of private generators should amount to 182.4 billion ID. As with large generators, we assume a value-added-to-output ratio of 40 percent.

Results

Table 5.1 presents value added estimates for each type of entity. Value added is estimated to be 555.9 billion ID (447.5 million USD). Appendix C presents more detailed calculations for distribution and large generators.

Discussion

As noted above, we faced a number of challenges in estimating value added from electricity, the two most important of which were:

- We were unable to obtain data on intermediate consumption for large generators, and thus relied on an assumption about the ratio of value-added-to-output drawn from European industry estimates.

Table 5.1
Value Added by Electricity Sector (ID, billions)

Type of Entity	Value Added
Distribution by the MoE	256.2
Large generators	226.7
Small private generators	73.0
Total	555.9

[2] We used the European average, given a lack of information on the Middle East and North Africa region. Since the value added to gross output ratio is likely to reflect the fuel mix used in generating electricity, which will vary by country and region, in future years it would be better to obtain data on intermediate consumption directly from generators in the KRI.

[3] This number is an average of the reported price of ID 6,000 in wintertime and ID 2,500 in summertime.

[4] Estimated using KRG's 2012 population figure of 5,059,010 and the ratio of population-to-households in the KRI from the 2012 Iraq Household Socio-Economic Survey (IHSES), equaling 5.6574 (5,158,948/911,892).

- We were unable to obtain data on small generation output or intermediate consumption, and thus relied on a variety of estimates of probable use levels, based on our discussions with KRSO staff.

It is not clear whether our assumptions are likely to lead to an underestimate or overestimate of value added from this sector.

CHAPTER SIX

Construction

This chapter presents estimates for value added from the construction sector, based on data and information from a variety of sources.

Construction activities in the KRI are carried out by two kinds of entities: firms and households. Construction firms (contractors) typically work for larger clients, such as businesses, institutions, and government. Our discussions with KRSO staff suggest that, in some cases, higher-income households may hire construction firms to perform new construction or renovation. Most households, however, undertake these activities on their own, buying materials and hiring labor. Therefore, the analysis of the GRP contribution of the construction sector must account for the activities of households and construction firms; the former are referred to as "owner construction."

Methods

Owner Construction

Any household carrying out a construction project for itself is legally required to obtain a permit for this work. The KRSO provided us with the lists of permits (one list for each governorate) for the year 2012. We considered using the production approach to calculate value added for this sector, but data availability made this challenging. Specifically, implementing the production approach would involve multiplying the number of square meters of construction (from the permit lists) by the market value of housing per square meter to obtain total market value, then applying an estimate of value-added-to-output. However, we were unable to obtain reliable data on market value per square meter, particularly since these estimates would need to be disaggregated enough to reflect important differences in the value of new construction across governorates and between rural and urban areas within governorates.

Therefore, we used the income approach by summing payments made by the household to labor hired for the construction. In principle, capital depreciation should be included as well; however, depreciation is not relevant in this case, since households generally do not use significant quantities of capital goods of their own for this activity.

The income approach, though preferable, posed significant challenges as well. While we obtained data on the total cost of construction from the list of permits from 2012, these data did not break down costs into materials versus hired labor.[1] KRSO staff provided us with

[1] A potential challenge is that some individuals may have carried out construction activities without obtaining permits, leading to an underestimate of value added from this sector.

rough estimates of the proportion of the costs attributable to labor in the three stages of construction, as follows:

- First stage: constructing the frame. Labor is estimated to account for around 5–7 percent of total cost for this stage, with the rest of the cost attributable to materials.
- Second stage: installing electricity, piping, etc. Labor is estimated to account for around 30–35 percent of total cost for this stage.
- Third stage: finishing the building. Labor is estimated to account for around 50 percent of total cost for this stage.

We were unable to identify what fraction of the overall cost was attributable to each stage. However, KRSO staff indicated that the second stage would take the longest amount of time; therefore, we assumed that it would account for 50 percent of total cost, with the first and third stages accounting for 25 percent each.

Firm Construction

The best source of information for construction activities by construction firms is an enterprise survey. There were no recent survey data for such enterprises in the KRI, so a new survey was developed for this project.

The sampling frame for the survey is the up-to-date ministry listing of all registered construction firms. The KRSO collected this information in January 2014. The total number of firms by governorate is 1,326 in Erbil, 1,077 in Sulaymaniyah, and 657 in Duhok. From this list, we drew a random sample of 1,620 enterprises, stratified by governorate. We performed statistical power calculations to determine the desired number of firms needed to obtain value added estimates with the desired precision. These calculations require information on firms' output or value added (see discussion in Appendix F). Since we lack direct information on this for construction firms, we used data from the recent internal trade survey, which also informed the calculations for the new services survey, to determine the necessary sample size. Based on these calculations, the selected sample includes 702 firms from Erbil, 570 from Sulaymaniyah, and 348 from Duhok. We used the remaining enterprises in the ministry listings for each governorate to draw replacement firms as needed.

We reviewed the sampling strategy and questionnaire with KRSO staff, including managers from KRSO offices in each governorate, during a trip in early February 2014, and made adjustments to the questionnaire. The format of the questionnaire was similar to the services questionnaire discussed in detail in Chapter Twelve. However, the survey also included a few questions particular to the construction industry. For example, on the revenue side, information was collected on income from building and construction services to clients as well as revenue from providing labor services to other contractors. Similarly, on the expenditures side, the survey gathered information on payments made to other contractors, to capture the converse situation where the firm had hired other firms for specific tasks on its own projects. Also, given the highly seasonal nature of construction, questions on revenue and expenditures generally used the previous year rather than the previous month as the reference period. Respondents were therefore asked to provide information for the most recent completed calendar year (2013), but could choose a different reference period if needed. Most respondents provided data for calendar year 2013.

The questionnaire for construction firms can be seen in online Appendix G. Training of survey teams began in May 2014. Because of conditions on the ground during the summer of 2014, data collection was delayed, but the initial dataset was ready for analysis in August 2014.

After removing 11 duplicate records, the survey data contained results for 1,614 unique companies. However, only 1,165 of these were categorized as having completed the interview successfully. Of the others, many declined the interview or did not respond to all the questions required to calculate value added, and 110 were reported as closed or suspended and were not replaced. Of the 1,165 firms for which the interview was successfully completed, 480 were in Erbil, 403 were in Sulaymaniyah, and 282 were in Duhok. Table 6.1 shows the number of firms, number of sampled firms, and number of completed interviews by governorate.

We calculated value added as gross output minus intermediate consumption as follows:

Gross output =
Value of building and construction services
+ Sale of services to others
+ Net sale of buildings and land[2]
+ Sale of goods
+ Rental of buildings
+ Rental of other goods and machinery
+ Other revenues
+ Change in inventories of finished goods

Intermediate consumption =
Cost of goods and materials purchased for resale or for production
+ Payment to foreigner contractors
+ Rental of machines, equipment, and goods
+ Rental of building
+ Cost of water, electricity, communications services, and transportation
+ Cost of maintenance and repairing
+ Cost of legal services, advertising, insurance, and other services
+ Other costs
– Changes in inventories of raw materials and goods purchased for resale.

Table 6.1
Estimated Numbers of Firms, Sampled Firms, and Completed Surveys in the Construction Sector, 2014

	Duhok	Sulaymaniyah	Erbil	Total
Total (2014 listing)	657	1,077	1,326	3,060
Sampled	348	570	702	1,620
Completed interviews	282	403	480	1,165
Updated total number of firms (number of firms in 2014 listing × ratio of surviving firms)	631	1,022	1,197	2,850

SOURCE: Surveyed firm counts are based on the construction firm survey. Total firm counts are based on a 2014 listing provided by KRSO.

[2] This item was constructed as the sale of buildings (not included in the first item, "value of building and construction services" plus the sale of land, minus the purchase of land and buildings for resale).

The ministry listings compiled by the KRSO classified the firms into ten groups by size, plus one group that was unclassified, for a total of 11 groups. To make our estimates representative of the population of firms, we first calculated the fraction of operating firms versus total firms (including those reported closed or suspended), by class and governorate. We then multiplied this fraction by the total number of listed firms, to develop an estimate of the number of surviving firms in the population (2,850). We also created nonresponse weights by class and governorate. The resulting adjustment weights were extrapolated by a multiple to inflate our sample to the total number of estimated surviving firms. Finally, we applied these weights to the firm-level survey data to estimate total value added.

Preliminary results of value added estimates for firms showed three outlier firms contributing approximately 77 percent of the total value added for firm construction. While large values are possible, for these few firms the ratio of firm revenue (value of output) to expenditures was extraordinarily high, suggesting that one or the other quantities was misrecorded in the survey or represents a data entry error. We considered two methods for addressing these likely outliers:

1. Estimating value added by multiplying aggregate output at the governorate level by the employee-size class-weighted median of the ratio of value added to output for all firms in that governorate.
2. For firms with output-to-expenditure ratios in the top and bottom 1 percent of the distribution of this ratio, calculating value added by multiplying reported output by the weighted median ratio of value added to output for other firms in the same governorate (rather than calculating the value added by netting intermediate expenditures from output).

These strategies yielded similar results. We decided to calculate value added by taking the average of these two approaches for addressing outliers.

Results

Table 6.2 presents value added estimates for owner construction, based on the method discussed above. As shown in the next-to-last column, labor makes up slightly less than a third (32 percent) of the total cost of owner home construction. Value added is estimated to be 1.137 trillion ID (977 million USD).

Turning to valued added by construction by firms, Panels A and B of Table 6.3 present estimates of gross value added following the two approaches described above for addressing outliers. As noted above, we use an average of the two methods for the final value added; this is shown in Panel C. With this approach, value added by construction firms is estimated to be 3.994 trillion ID (3.43 billion USD).

Adding up the results for owner construction and firm construction, we estimate the value added by the construction sector to be 5.13 trillion ID (4.41 billion USD).

Table 6.2
Value Added of Owner Construction (ID, billions)

		Stage I (25%)		Stage II (50%)		Stage III (25%)			
Governorate	Total Cost	Total	Labor (7%)	Total	Labor (35%)	Total	Labor (50%)	Labor as % of Total Cost	Value Added
Erbil	2,072.8	518.2	36.3	1,036.4	362.7	518.2	259.1	31.8	658.1
Duhok	787.5	196.9	13.8	393.7	137.8	196.9	98.4	31.8	250.0
Sulaymaniyah	720.3	180.1	12.6	360.2	126.1	180.1	90.0	31.8	228.7
Total	3,580.6	895.2	62.7	1,790.3	626.6	895.2	447.6		1,136.8

Table 6.3
Value Added by Construction Firms (ID, billions)

Component	Erbil	Sulaymaniyah	Duhok
A: Value Added Estimated as Gross Output × Median Value Added to Output Ratio			
(1) Gross output	885.2	8,791.9	5,056.0
(2) Intermediate consumption	668.9	5,944.3	4,090.1
Median ratio (value added/output) across classes	0.2444	0.3239	0.1910
(3) Gross value added	216.3	2,847.6	965.9
Overall total	4,029.8		
B: Value Added Adjusted for Firms with Top and Bottom 1 Percent of Output-to-Expenditure Ratio			
(1) Gross output	885.2	8,791.9	5,056.0
(2) Intermediate consumption	669.6	5,626.7	4,479.7
(3) Gross value added (1 – 2)	215.6	3,165.3	576.3
Overall total	3,957.2		
C: Average of Two Methods for Addressing Outliers			
(1) Gross output	885.2	8,791.9	5,056.0
(2) Intermediate consumption	669.2	5,785.5	4,284.9
(3) Gross value added (1 – 2)	216.0	3,006.4	771.1
Overall total	3,993.5		

Discussion

Our estimates from owner construction, as discussed above, are based on a variety of assumptions on the relative costs of labor and materials in each stage of construction and on the share of each stage of construction in total costs. Based on our discussions with KRSO staff familiar with the construction sector, these assumptions appear to be reasonable. However, the estimates could in future be improved by collection of more complete data on housing values and owner construction costs.

As noted above, the sampling frame was developed in January 2014, and, given the need for accurate recall, we ask for information for calendar year 2013, not 2012. If the number of construction firms, or per-firm value added (or both), have been increasing as the KRI grows, the value added presented here may be an overestimate for 2012, the year for which we are calculating GRP.

CHAPTER SEVEN

Wholesale and Retail Trade

This chapter presents estimates for value added from the trading sector based on a survey conducted by the KRSO during 2012 and 2013.

Methods

The sampling frame for the survey was the 2009 census. Firms were surveyed from all three governorates of the KRI each month for a 12-month period (July 2012 to June 2013). The KRSO reported that individual firms may be in the dataset more than once.

The surveys covered major trade industries, classified in accordance with ISIC Revision 4 codes, at the four-digit level. The Wholesale and Retail Trade/Repair of Motor Vehicles and Motorcycles sector includes three broad (two-digit) classifications (45–47) and 20 three-digit classifications. Table 7.1 shows the number of firms and sampled firms for each three-digit classification by governorate. Retail sales (ISIC 47) account for 76 percent of firms in this sector.

We calculated value added as gross output minus intermediate consumption following UN guidance for industrial firms (United Nations, Department of Economic and Social Affairs, Statistics Division, 2008b), but modified to accommodate trading firms, as follows:

Gross output =
Value of shipments/turnover/sales of all goods and services purchased for resale in the same condition as received
– Purchases of goods and services for resale in the same condition as received
\+ Other revenues
\+ Change in inventories of goods purchased for resale in the same condition as received (closing – opening)

Intermediate consumption =
Cost of raw materials and supplies except gas, fuels and electricity
\+ Cost of gas, fuel and electricity purchased
\+ Cost of water and sewerage services
\+ Purchases of services except rental
\+ Rental payments.

To extrapolate the monthly survey data into yearly estimates, we multiplied each firm's gross output and intermediate consumption values by the number of months the firm operated

Table 7.1
Estimated Numbers of Firms and Sampled Firms in the Trade Sector, 2011

ISIC Revision 4 Code	Industry	Erbil		Sulaymaniyah		Duhok	
		Sampled	Total	Sampled	Total	Sampled	Total
451	Sale of Motor Vehicles	9	198	8	190	3	157
452	Maintenance and Repair of Motor Vehicles	107	3,945	116	4,069	51	1,838
453	Sale of Motor Vehicle Parts and Accessories	41	1,822	32	1,641	20	723
454	Sale, Maintenance and Repair of Motorcycles and Related Parts and Accessories	4	75	3	98	7	7
461	Wholesale on a Fee or Contract Basis	8	409	20	552	11	223
462	Wholesale of Agricultural Raw Materials and Live Animals	5	141	8	318	6	130
463	Wholesale of Food, Beverages and Tobacco	13	312	11	484	29	542
464	Wholesale of Household Goods	15	586	20	914	14	443
465	Wholesale of Machinery, Equipment and supplies	2	147	6	196	3	120
466	Other Specialized Wholesale	20	657	56	1,043	22	495
469	Non-Specialized Wholesale Trade	1	53	2	55	3	36
471	Retail Sale in Non-Specialized Stores	141	5,687	155	6,813	103	4,404
472	Retail Sale of Food, Beverages and Tobacco in Specialized Stores	187	4,809	228	9,472	90	3,778
473	Retail Sale of Automotive Fuel in Specialized Stores	31	642	34	702	5	171
474	Retail Sale of Information and Communications Equipment in Specialized Stores	27	1,187	28	1,345	16	738
475	Retail Sale of Other Household Equipment in Specialized Stores	145	4,051	154	4,845	71	2,462
476	Retail Sale of Cultural and Recreation Goods in Specialized Stores	25	695	21	1,079	10	350
477	Retail Sale of Other Goods in Specialized Stores	134	5,719	151	7,789	82	3,888
478	Retail Sale via Stalls and Markets	3	159	3	155	5	250
479	Retail Trade Not in Stores, Stalls or Markets	1	42	6	9	5	6
	Other (ISIC blank or not valid)	49	–	9	–	8	–
	Total	968	31,336	1,071	41,769	564	20,761

SOURCE: Surveyed firm counts are based on counts from the firm-level datasets. Total firm counts are based on the 2009 census.

(obtained by using the survey question of which months the firm stopped work). All but 19 firms reported being operational all 12 months of the year.[1]

In addition, to arrive at the value added for the population of firms (rather than the sample), the value added for each three-digit ISIC code value was multiplied by the ratio of the total number of firms in that three-digit ISIC code (from the 2009 sampling frame) to the number of firms sampled (see Table 7.1) to get the total value.[2]

Results

Table 7.2 presents estimates of gross value added (equal to gross output minus intermediate consumption), which amounts to 2,499 billion ID (2.15 billion USD). Appendix D presents more details on methodology and estimates by ISIC code.

Table 7.2
Value Added by Wholesale and Retail Trading Sector (ID, billions)

Component	Erbil	Sulaymaniyah	Duhok
(1) Gross output	10,269	5,932	4,798
(2) Intermediate consumption	9,104	5,104	4,291
(3) Gross value added (1 – 2)	1,165	828	507
Overall total	2,499		

Discussion

The key challenge associated with trading sector data (as with manufacturing sector data) is that the sampling frame was based on the 2009 census. It is likely that the number of trading firms has risen since 2009, given overall growth in the KRI, so that our estimates understate value added in 2012; that is, when expanding the value added per firm by total number of firms in the census to get aggregate value added for the sector, we may be multiplying by too small a number of firms.

On the other hand, the trading survey was conducted not during calendar year 2012 but rather July 2012 through June 2013. To the extent that value added per firm has been increasing, the use of a later (but overlapping) period for the survey implies that our estimates may overstate value added for 2012.

On balance, we suspect that our estimates are more likely to underestimate value added in 2012, given the period of time elapsed between the census and the survey and the likely growth in the size of the population of trading enterprises over time.

[1] Most firms reported operating for a full 12 months. Although the survey covered July 2012 through June 2013, we did not confine the analysis to only the six months in calendar year 2012 (for which we want to construct the GRP estimate), because we were concerned about the seasonality in construction. Therefore, we included all 12 months even though for six of these months the data were from 2013.

[2] We dropped firms with missing ISIC codes, as we were unable to estimate an appropriate inflation factor from the 2009 sampling frame.

CHAPTER EIGHT

Transportation and Storage

This chapter presents estimates for value added from the transportation and storage sector. The results are based largely on a new survey of transportation and storage firms, as described below. However, we also separately included value added from airports.

Methods

Airports

To estimate the value added generated at the KRI's airports (Erbil International Airport and Sulaymaniyah International Airport), we obtained the total number of air passengers in the KRI, as well as an estimated value added per passenger. We obtained the number of passenger flights from the 2012 air transport survey report, which indicated that there were 1,236,742 passengers in 2012.

We derived value added per passenger from research on India's Delhi Airport (National Council of Applied Economic Research, 2012). Delhi Airport serves as a useful comparison, given that its level of technological development and economic efficiency are reasonably similar to those of the KRI. According to the National Council of Applied Economic Research, in 2009–2010 Delhi Airport generated value added of about 38,412 ID (33 USD) per passenger, which we multiply by the number of passengers in the KRI to derive total value added.

Transportation and Storage Firms

A host of small firms operate in the transportation sector of the KRI economy, including trucking, passenger transport, and various activities in support of transportation. Many of these are very small enterprises. The 2009 KRI census counted 2,775 transportation enterprises. Even more numerous are enterprises involved in the related activity of storage and warehousing (more than 10,000). As there was no recent survey of the transportation and storage sector, these activities were included as part of the new services survey for calculations of GRP using the census as the sampling frame. Details of the survey, including sampling strategy, sample size considerations, and timing, are discussed in Chapter Twelve. The sample size for transportation and storage combined was 1,626 enterprises. The survey instrument used for transportation and storage enterprises was almost the same as that for other service enterprises (presented in online Appendix G), but included a separate section on vehicles and storage facilities owned or rented by the enterprise.

As with the construction survey, the transportation and storage survey was conducted during the spring of 2014. Since this sector is dominated by numerous small firms, RAND

and the KRSO judged it likely that many of these firms would not keep formal accounts and so would be unable to provide accurate revenue and expenditure information for an annual reference period. Therefore, respondents were asked to report revenue and cost information for the previous month, but they could select a different reference period (including the past year) if desired. Most respondents reported information from December 2013.

The survey data for the transportation and storage sector contained results for 1,605 unique companies, 1,528 of which consisted of complete interviews. Of these 1,528 firms, 504 were located in Erbil, 652 in Sulaymaniyah, and 372 in Duhok. Table 8.1 shows the number of firms, number of sampled firms, and number of completed interviews, by sector and governorate.

We calculated value added as gross output minus intermediate consumption as follows:

Gross output =
Sale of services
+ Sale of goods
+ Rental of buildings
+ Rental of other capital and goods
+ Other revenues
+ Change in inventories of finished goods

Intermediate consumption =
Cost of goods and materials purchased for resale or for production
+ Cost of water, electricity, communications services, and transportation
+ Rental of building and offices
+ Rental of machines, equipment, and goods
+ Cost of maintenance and repairing
+ Cost of legal services, advertising, insurance, and other services
+ Other costs
– Changes in inventories of raw materials and goods purchased for resale.

Because of the (relatively small) differences between the intended sample and the number of successfully interviewed firms, we calculated nonresponse weights by activity and governorate. The resulting adjustment weights were extrapolated by a multiple to reach the total number of firms in the sector in the KRI based on the census (12,893).

Table 8.1
Estimated Numbers of Firms and Sampled Firms in the Transportation and Storage Sectors, 2014

	Transportation			Storage			
	Duhok	Sulaymaniyah	Erbil	Duhok	Sulaymaniyah	Erbil	Total
Total	1,206	683	886	2,196	4,755	3,167	12,893
Sample	152	86	112	277	600	399	1,626
Successfully interviewed	95	100	130	277	552	374	1,528

SOURCE: Surveyed firm counts are based on counts from the services firm survey. Total firm counts are based on the 2009 census.

Preliminary estimates indicated that one outlier firm reported huge losses, resulting in negative value added for the sector as a whole. We were not able to ascertain whether the large losses represented a reporting or a recording mistake. Thus, we followed the same strategy for addressing outliers as for construction firms (see Chapter Six).

Results

Airports

Multiplying the number of passengers in the KRI in 2012 by estimated per-passenger value added resulted in an estimated value added of 47.2 billion ID (41 million USD).

Transportation and Storage Firms

Table 8.2 presents estimates of gross value added following the two approaches for addressing outliers in Panels A and B. As noted above, we use an average of the two methods to estimate final value added, shown in Panel C. Value added is estimated to be 1.71 trillion ID in 2012 (1.465 billion USD).

Total value added for the transportation and storage sector, including the surveys and airports, is estimated to be 1.75 trillion ID in 2012 (1.51 billion USD).

Table 8.2
Value Added by Transportation and Storage Surveys (ID, billions)

Component	Erbil	Sulaymaniyah	Duhok
A: Value Added Estimated as Gross Output × Median Value Added to Output Ratio			
(1) Gross output	609.9	1,771.6	4,528.4
(2) Intermediate consumption	362.9	1,299.4	3,446.6
Median ratio (value added/output) across classes	0.4050	0.2665	0.2388
(3) Gross value added	247.0	472.2	1,081.8
Overall total	1,801.1		
B: Value Added Adjusted for Firms with Top and Bottom 1 Percent of Output-to-Expenditure Ratio			
(1) Gross output	609.9	1,771.6	4,528.4
(2) Intermediate consumption	384.3	1,253.4	3,662.0
(3) Gross value added (1 – 2)	225.6	518.2	866.4
Overall total	1,610.3		
C: Average of Two Methods for Addressing Outliers			
(1) Gross output	609.9	1,771.6	4,528.4
(2) Intermediate consumption	373.6	1,276.4	3,554.3
(3) Gross value added (1 – 2)	236.3	495.2	974.1
Overall total	1,705.7		

Discussion

The estimate for value added from airports relies on per-passenger value added from Delhi Airport. We used this per-passenger value because the level of development in Delhi makes it a reasonable comparison for the KRI. In addition, we note that our estimates for value added from this sector are missing any value added from airlines themselves. We were unable to obtain data from the airports and airlines directly, and the estimate for value added from this sector could be improved in the future by doing so.

In the case of transportation and storage, there are two key challenges associated with the analysis. First, the survey data for one firm indicated huge losses that may represent a reporting or recording error in the field or a data entry error. Our value added estimates followed two reasonable approaches to address this and other outliers. Second, the list of firms was based on a 2009 sampling frame. It is likely that the number of transportation and storage firms has risen since 2009, given overall growth in the KRI.

In addition, the suspension of revenue transfers from Baghdad to the KRG during the survey period likely had some dampening impact on overall economic activity, reflected in recorded activity and revenues below normal levels. Our calculations are thus likely to slightly underestimate value added by this sector in 2012. At the same time, most survey respondents provided information on costs and revenues from December 2013, and if per-firm value added has risen over time, our calculations may overestimate value added for 2012. On balance, we suspect it is more likely that the former effect dominates, and our calculations likely represent a lower bound on value added for this sector in 2012.

CHAPTER NINE

Accommodation and Food Service

This chapter presents estimates for value added from restaurants and hotels, based on surveys conducted by the KRSO and the CSO.

Methods

Hotels

Value added from hotels is based on a 2012 survey of hotel and accommodation activities. We obtained survey data for Erbil and Sulaymaniyah governorates and a summary report for Duhok governorate from the KRSO. The KRSO indicated that the survey was a census of all hotels, motels, and tourist complexes. The data and report indicate that there were 614 hotels in the KRI (251 hotels in Erbil, 154 in Sulaymaniyah, and 209 in Duhok).

When calculating output of hotels, one must distinguish between two types of activities. First, hotels provide accommodation services (short-term rental of rooms and related tourist services), for which all activity-related revenues are counted as output. Second, hotels also engage in resale of previously bought food or beverages. This latter activity is treated as distributive trade, and output in this case equals only the trade margin, which is the difference between sales (revenues) and cost of goods bought. In this case, the output also includes changes in inventories, as in the wholesale trade sector.

We estimated intermediate consumption by summing expenditures on commodity supplies (for example, fuel, gas, spare parts) and services (for example, advertising, legal services). We then estimated value added using the production approach.

Restaurants

We received survey data from the KRSO for a 2014 survey of restaurants and coffee shops, conducted by the CSO and the KRSO. The restaurant survey was reported to include a representative sample of firms. The data included sampling multipliers, which we used to arrive at an estimate of value added for the population of restaurants. Applying the sampling multipliers indicates that the population of restaurants in the KRI was 5,814 (4,735 restaurants in Sulaymaniyah, 429 in Erbil, and 650 in Duhok).[1]

We estimated restaurant output by summing all activity-related revenues. Intermediate consumption was estimated as the sum of expenditures on food and beverage and other goods

[1] The large number of restaurants in Sulaymaniyah, relative to the other two governorates, is surprising, but is confirmed by the counts from the sampling frames for each governorate. As noted in Chapter Fifteen, the proposed enterprise census should help to update and verify the correct number of restaurants for future estimates.

and services purchased (for example, electricity, gas, water, rent). We then estimated value added using the production approach. We applied the sampling weights provided in the data to estimate value added for the population.

Results

Tables 9.1 and 9.2 present estimates of gross value added for hotels and food service (equal to gross output minus intermediate consumption). For hotels, value added amounts to 193.1 billion ID (165.9 million USD). For restaurants, value added amounts to 661.4 billion ID (568.2 million USD).[2] The total value added by hotels and restaurants is estimated to be 854.5 billion ID in 2012 (0.73 billion USD).

Table 9.1
Value Added by Hotels (ID, billions)

Component	Erbil	Sulaymaniyah	Duhok
(1) Gross output	198.4	33.5	16.7
(2) Intermediate consumption	40.3	11.0	4.2
(3) Gross value added (1 – 2)	158.1	22.5	12.5
Overall total	193.1		

Table 9.2
Value Added by Restaurants (ID, billions)

Component	Erbil	Sulaymaniyah	Duhok
(1) Gross output	194.9	935.8	267.5
(2) Intermediate consumption	100.5	509.7	126.6
(3) Gross value added (1 – 2)	94.4	426.1	140.9
Overall total	661.4		

Discussion

Since the hotel survey was a census of all hotels in the KRI, sampling issues do not arise for this subsector. It is possible that the survey missed some hotels, in which case value added may be understated to some extent.

Two potential challenges should be noted with respect to the restaurant survey. First, the survey was conducted in 2014. We would typically expect value added to be higher in later years; however, given the disruptions that occurred in the KRI in 2014, it is possible that restaurant value added was lower in this year than in 2012. Second, it is not clear when the sampling frame was updated, which may tend to understate value added if new restaurants were not added.

[2] We compared our value added estimates for restaurants against a CSO report of value added. The CSO reported value added of 99.5 billion ID for Erbil, 468.8 billion ID for Sulaymaniyah, and 148.6 billion ID for Duhok. The reason for the slightly higher numbers from the CSO report are unclear, but if we were to use the reported numbers, the total value added from restaurants would be 716.9 billion ID (about 8 percent higher than our estimates).

CHAPTER TEN

Information and Communications (Large Firms)

This chapter presents estimates for value added for large firms in the information and communications sector based on a compilation of data from interviews and publicly available reports. Smaller firms in this sector were covered as part of the miscellaneous services survey (see Chapter Twelve).

Methods

The information and communications sector is dominated by a few large firms, which contribute a large share of sectoral output. To avoid missing these firms because of the sampling process used in the miscellaneous services survey, we supplemented that survey with publicly available information on, and interviews with, large firms.

First, we obtained information on large telecommunications firms. The three main telecommunications firms in Iraq are Asiacell, Korek Telecom, and Zain Iraq (Invest in Group, 2013). Zain Iraq is based in Baghdad and operates largely in southern and central Iraq, so in estimating KRI's GRP we focused on contributions from Asiacell and Korek. For Asiacell, we obtained information on revenues and expenses from the firm's 2012 annual report and estimated its total value added using the production approach (Asiacell Communications PJSC–Sulaymaniyah, 2013). To estimate the share of Asiacell's value added attributable to the KRI, we multiplied the firm's total value added by the fraction of employees reported to be in the KRI.[1]

For Korek, we searched for, but were unable to obtain, publicly available information on revenues and expenditures. Therefore, we estimated value added for Korek by multiplying the estimated value added per subscriber for Asiacell (154,812 ID per subscriber or 133 USD per subscriber) by Korek's number of subscribers.[2] Since Korek is based in the KRI, we assumed that all value added accrued to the region.

Second, KRSO staff conducted interviews with four large media firms (newspapers, magazines, radio). We note that a drawback of these interviews is that they were conducted in 2014, so they may reflect a larger number of employees than would have been present in 2012, if

[1] Employee share may not be a good indicator of value added share if employment is concentrated in one location but profit-generating activities occur in other locations, as may be the case in this industry. Unfortunately, in the absence of information on revenue share attributable to the KRI, we have no recourse but to use employment share.

[2] We obtained information about the number of subscribers from Invest in Group (2013). Asiacell was reported to have approximately 10 million subscribers throughout Iraq, while Korek was reported to have approximately 4.8 million. We were unable to obtain information on what shares of these subscribers were inside the KRI.

media firms have been growing over time as KRI develops. We initially attempted to estimate value added using a production approach. However, the revenue information we received did not appear to be complete, so we used an income approach instead. To do so, we multiplied the reported number of employees by average annual employee wages (8.1 million ID) for the media sector (taken from the 2013 Kurdistan Region Labor Force Survey conducted by the KRSO).[3] We also estimated the consumption of fixed capital to account for approximately 5 percent of value added, based on a review of countries that are at a similar stage of economic development to that of the KRI.

Results

The value added to the KRI in 2012 was estimated to be 1.844 trillion ID (1.58 billion USD) (Table 10.1).

Table 10.1
Value Added by Large Firms in Information and Communications Sector (ID, billions)

Entity	Value Added
(1) Asiacell	1,102.7
(2) Korek	740.5
(3) Other large firms	1.1
Overall total	1,844.3

Discussion

Value added in the information and communications sector is highly skewed toward the largest firms. Since we were able to obtain an annual report for Asiacell, we have confidence in the value added estimates for this firm. Korek presented a greater challenge, since our estimates assume that value added per subscriber is the same as that of Asiacell, and also that the estimates of numbers of subscribers were reasonable for 2012. Future estimates of value added in this sector could be improved by obtaining information directly from these two firms.

[3] We calculated wages using the 2013 Kurdistan Region Labor Force Survey because this was the year of the survey for which the most complete data were available.

CHAPTER ELEVEN

Banking, Insurance, and Money Exchanges

This chapter presents estimates for value added for banks, insurance companies, and money exchanges. Other financial service firms were covered as part of the miscellaneous services survey (see Chapter Twelve).

Methods

Banks

We followed the income approach to estimate value added for banks, in keeping with common practice in developing countries. To do so, we summed up total salaries, operational surplus (net profits), and depreciation or consumption of fixed capital. The banking sector in the KRI is composed of four types of entities: government-owned "trade" banks, local private banks based in the KRI, banks based in the rest of Iraq (headquartered in Baghdad) with branches in the KRI, and foreign banks. Below, we provide further details on value added calculations for each type of bank.

Government-Owned Trade Banks

We obtained limited information on government-owned trade banks from the CSO. We calculated value added by summing up the total salary expenditures (including income tax and retirement contributions) paid by the 79 branches of government-owned trade banks. Profits were reported to be zero, given that these are government institutions. We were not able to obtain data on consumption of fixed capital, so this element is not included in our calculations.

Local Private Banks

Only three local banks operate in the KRI: Kurdistan Investment Bank (KIBID), Cihan Bank, and Erbil Bank. For both KIBID and Cihan Bank, we used 2012 financial reports to estimate value added by summing salaries and wages, operational surplus (profits), and depreciation.[1] For Erbil Bank, for which we were unable to obtain a financial report, we used a report provided by the CSO to obtain data for 2011. We then inflated the information for 2012, assuming growth equal to the average growth recorded for KIBID and Cihan Banks (83 percent).

In estimating the KRI's GRP, it is necessary to take into account only the share of value added that is actually generated in the KRI, rather than in other parts of Iraq or abroad. KIBID's financial report indicates that it has one branch outside of the KRI, based in Bagh-

[1] As a check, we also estimated 2011 value added using data from the 2012 financial reports. The 2011 figures were in line with figures provided separately by the CSO.

dad, and that this branch is responsible for 8.55 percent of KIBID's total profit. Similarly, Cihan Bank's financial report indicates that 23.59 percent of its profit is generated by its Baghdad branch. Hence, we allocate only 91.45 percent and 76.41 percent, respectively, of KIBID's and Cihan Bank's value added to the KRI's GRP. For Erbil bank, we assume that the KRI's share is the average of shares reported by KIBID and Cihan (84 percent).

Iraqi Private Banks

There are 24 banks based in the rest of Iraq that operate in the KRI. The CSO provided estimates of 2011 value added for 21 of these banks, which we use for estimating GRP.[2] The value added by these banks in 2011 equaled 413.9 billion ID (356 million USD). To inflate these figures for 2012, we used the reported nominal growth of the banking and insurance sector for all of Iraq, which amounted to 30.43 percent.[3] This brought the value added of the private Iraqi banks operating in the KRI to a total of 540 ID billion (463 million USD) (see Table E.2).

We were unable to obtain information on the share of value added or employment attributable to branches in the KRI. To address this issue, we developed an estimate of this share based on previous estimates of the KRI's GRP (van Tongeren and Bartlema, 2010). Previous estimates suggested that the KRI's non-oil GRP was 20,954 billion ID in 2008, and that the banking and insurance sector accounted for approximately 1.3 percent of value added. Given that banks and insurance constituted 1.51 percent of Iraq's GDP in 2009,[4] and that the KRI's non-oil GRP is roughly 25 percent of total Iraq's non-oil GDP, we estimated that the KRI's banking and insurance share was roughly 21.5 percent (25 percent × [1.3/1.51]). Using this informed guess, we attributed 116 billion ID (100 million USD) of private Iraqi banks' value added to the KRI.

Foreign Banks

According to the KRI's central bank, ten foreign banks operate in the KRI. We obtained estimates of value added for three of them—Beirut Bank, Vakiflar Bank, and Turkish Agricultural Bank—in 2011, from the CSO.[5] We assumed that the value added for the remaining seven banks was zero, as they appeared to be newly established banks without substantial value added at this time.

To determine the share of value added attributable to the KRI, we examined each bank's branch locations. Vakiflar Bank's operations in Iraq include only one branch in Erbil, so we assumed that all of its value added was within the KRI. Both Beirut Bank and Turkish Agricultural Bank have one branch in Erbil and one in Baghdad—hence we assumed that 50 percent of their value added was attributable to the KRI. We then inflated the 2011 values to 2012, assuming the same bank growth rate as for local private banks (83 percent).

---

[2] Two additional banks appear to have insignificant operations in the KRI; we were unable to find further information about their operations in the KRI. A third bank was classified by the CSO as foreign and reported negative value added. We excluded these three banks from our calculations.

[3] According to the CSO, nominal GDP of the banking and insurance sector in Iraq grew from 2,779,312.2 million ID to 3,625,093.8 million ID (2.4 to 3.1 billion USD) between 2011 and 2012. See CSO, no date.

[4] Iraq's total GDP, excluding crude oil, was reported as 74.6 trillion ID (64 billion USD) in 2009. See CSO, no date.

[5] We excluded CSO data that included negative figures, since these are unsustainable figures that would likely be reversed in later years.

Insurance Companies

The insurance sector in the KRI is characterized by a small private sector and three large, publicly owned institutions headquartered in Baghdad. We estimated value added for the private institutions based on information from interviews with the three main private insurance companies in the KRI—Ur, Star, and Asia. For Asia and Ur, we calculated value added based on the income approach, by summing profits and salaries. Star supplied only revenue data, so we assumed it had a value-added-to-revenue ratio equal to the average of the ratio calculated for the other two companies and used this to calculate value added.

For the public-sector institutions, we received information from three companies—the National Insurance Company, the Iraqi Insurance Company, and the Iraqi Reinsurance Company—for 2011. We used a top-down approach, attributing a share of the Iraqi-wide value added to the KRI. We attributed 21.5 percent of the Iraqi-wide value added to the KRI, based on the percentage used for Iraqi private banks. We assumed that value added did not change between 2011 and 2012.

Money Exchanges

The KRSO and the CSO fielded a survey of money transfer and exchange facilities operating in 2012 across all of Iraq, including in the KRI. We obtained a summary of the results, including a calculation of value added by governorate. The calculation is supported through both a production approach and an income approach, as we were given information on output, intermediate consumption, product taxes and fees, as well as information on compensation of employees and operating surplus.

Results

The value added to the KRI in 2012 was estimated to be 269.5 billion ID from banks, 16.2 billion ID from insurance companies, and 19.5 billion ID from money exchanges, for a total of 305.3 billion ID (262.3 million USD) (Table 11.1). Appendix E presents more details on calculations for banks and money exchanges.

Table 11.1
Value Added by Financial Sector (ID, billions)

Category	Value Added
Banks	269.6
Government-owned trade banks	48.5
Local private banks	102.5
Iraqi private banks	116.1
Foreign banks	2.5
Insurance companies	16.2
Money exchanges	19.5
Overall total	305.3

FISIM

Banks and other financial institutions charge a value for their services that is implicit in the interest rates faced by borrowers and lenders. These services, known as financial intermediation services indirectly measured (FISIM), must be netted out of gross value added. In practice, FISIM can be estimated as the difference between interest received from loans and interest paid on deposits. It is recommended (*System of National Accounts 2008*, 2009) that FISIM be allocated as inputs to industries (including public administration) and households, and only the portion of FISIM allocated as inputs to industries be netted out. However, while we have data on total interest received and paid, we do not have the additional information on loans and deposits that would be required to allocate FISIM across industries and households, nor do we observe explicit service charges. Thus, we follow earlier *System of National Accounts 1993* guidance and treat all FISIM as if it were allocated to industries. Details on FISIM estimates are provided in Appendix E. Using this method, we estimate FISIM to be 58.4 billion ID (50.2 million USD).

Discussion

Our value added estimates for the banking, insurance, and money exchanges sector are compiled from a variety of sources and are based largely on the income approach. The two critical assumptions we made in many of our estimates were (1) the fraction of value added attributable to the KRI, and (2) the rate of growth in value added between 2011 and 2012. Where data were available, we based our assumptions for these two factors on similar firms. Despite all the assumptions we make, the 1.1 percent of value added by this sector to the entire economy is very similar to the 1.3 percent estimate for 2008 mentioned above. Future estimates of value added can be improved by directly collecting more detailed, up-to-date data.

CHAPTER TWELVE

Miscellaneous Services

The KRSO has implemented surveys (sometimes in collaboration with the CSO) for several key activities in the service sector. These surveys provide the necessary information to calculate value added. These activities include internal trade, restaurants and cafes, hotels, and money exchanges. However, a number of other service activities are not covered by these surveys, such as transportation and storage services (discussed in Chapter Eight) and the following additional service activities:

1. Information and Communications (specifically, book publishing, newspapers, computer programming, consultancy, and related activities; and information services). While the category includes large telecommunications companies, television, radio, and recording firms as well as large publishers, a subset of these large firms was covered separately through interviews and collection of publicly available data).[1]
2. Finance and Insurance
3. Real Estate
4. Professional, Scientific and Technical Activities
5. Human Health and Social Work Activities
6. Administrative and Support Services Activities
7. Arts, Entertainment and Recreation
8. Other Service Activities.

Most of these activities individually make up only a small portion of all services and, even more so, of overall GRP. Together, however, they become significant. Unlike the sectors already covered by recent surveys and the new construction enterprise survey described in Chapter Six, there are generally no up-to-date lists of enterprises collected by relevant ministries for these various activities that can be used as a sampling frame for new surveys. In part, this is a reflection of the fact that many of these subsectors are, relatively speaking, small in number. Given the lack of available up-to-date listings of enterprises from other sources, we rely on the 2009 census as the sampling frame for the survey of the activities listed above as well as the survey of transportation and storage firms. We discuss the sampling approach in Appendix F.

[1] Specifically, KRSO staff interviewed two newspaper publishers, one magazine publisher, and one radio broadcasting firm. In addition, we estimated value added for two large telecommunications firms based on publicly available information. Value added for these firms is reported in Chapter Ten.

Methods

Survey of Services Firms

As noted in Chapter Eight, the services survey included transportation and storage activities as well as other service activities. The results for transportation and storage were presented in Chapter Eight; here we present results for other service activities.

As with the transportation/storage survey, the services survey was conducted in spring 2014. As with the transportation/storage sector, the services sector is dominated by numerous small firms, many of which do not keep formal accounts and so would be unable to provide accurate revenue and expenditure information for an annual reference period. Therefore, respondents were asked to report revenue and cost information for the previous month, but they could select a different reference period if preferred. Most respondents reported information from December 2013.

Out of the 1,628 firms listed in the intended sample of firms performing other (nontransportation, nonstorage) activities, we received information for 1,598 firms, of which 1,572 successfully completed interviews. Of these 1,572 firms, 585 were in Erbil, 676 were in Sulaymaniyah, and 311 were in Duhok. Table 12.1 shows the number of firms that completed interviews by sector and governorate.

We calculated value added as gross output minus intermediate consumption as follows:

Gross output =
Sale of services
+ Sale of goods
+ Rental of buildings
+ Rental of other capital or goods
+ Other revenues
+ Change in inventories of finished goods

Table 12.1
Estimated Numbers of Firms Successfully Interviewed in Other Service Activities, 2014

Sector	Duhok	Sulaymaniyah	Erbil	Total
Information and communications	12	36	31	79
Financial and insurance	12	21	17	50
Real estate	39	58	63	160
Professional, technical, and scientific	98	87	70	255
Administrative and support services	36	110	103	249
Human health and social work	7	24	16	47
Arts, entertainment, and recreation	28	43	32	103
Other services	79	297	253	629
Total	311	676	585	1,572

SOURCE: Services firm survey.

Intermediate consumption =
Cost of goods and materials purchased for resale or for production
+ Cost of water, electricity, communications services, and transportation
+ Rental of building and offices
+ Rental of machines, equipment, and goods
+ Cost of maintenance and repairing
+ Cost of legal services, advertising, insurance, and other services
+ Other costs
– Changes in inventories of raw materials and goods purchased for resale.

Because of the difference between the intended sample and the number of successfully interviewed firms, we calculated nonresponse weights by sector and governorate. The resulting adjustment weights were extrapolated by a multiple to reach the total number of firms in the KRI (20,065).

As with construction and transportation/storage, we found several outlier values in the dataset. To address these outliers, we applied the same methodology, using the average of two methods as described in Chapter Six.

Interviews with Larger Services Firms

In addition to thousands of small and medium-sized firms, the services sector includes a smaller number of larger enterprises, particularly in the education and health areas (namely, schools and hospitals). While small in number, such enterprises contribute disproportionately to value added due to their size. Because of the random sampling process used in the miscellaneous services survey, these relatively rare large enterprises will generally be missed by the survey, which consequently will miss a significant part of the value added in the sectors involved. Therefore, we supplemented the survey with interviews with hospitals and schools. Only private schools and hospitals were included, since public institutions are covered under the public administration sector (Chapter Thirteen).

KRSO staff conducted interviews with two large hospitals. We also obtained a list of the number of beds in each of the largest private hospitals. The list included 43 private health institutions with a total of 646 beds. We calculated the value added generated per bed for the two hospitals with which the KRSO conducted interviews; these values were quite similar (approximately 28 million ID or 24,000 USD per bed). We then extrapolated this value to the total number of beds in the list, using value added from each of the two hospitals that were interviewed, and took an average of the two estimates.

The KRSO also conducted an interview with one private school. We also obtained a list of the number of students in each of the largest private schools. In the interview with the school, we did not obtain sufficient information to calculate value added using a production approach. Thus, as with the media sector, we used an income approach instead. To do so, we multiplied the reported number of teachers by the average annual wage (8.6 million ID or 7,400 USD) for employees in the education sector in 2013 (taken from the Kurdistan Region Labor Force Survey). We also estimated the consumption of fixed capital to account for approximately 5 percent of value added, based on a review of countries that are at a similar stage of economic development to that of the KRI. We then extrapolated this value to the total number of students in the list of private schools.

Results

Surveys of Services Firms

Table 12.2 presents estimates of gross value added following the two approaches for addressing outliers in Panels A and B. As noted above, we use an average of the two methods for the final value added, shown in Panel C. Value added is estimated to be 1.966 trillion ID (1.69 billion USD). Table 12.3 presents average gross value added by activity.

Interviews with Services Firms

Table 12.4 presents estimates of gross value added for large private hospitals, based on the method described above. As noted above, we estimate value added based on the value added generated per bed of the two hospitals, and take an average of the two estimates. Value added is estimated to be 18.0 billion ID (0.016 billion USD).

For large schools, we extrapolated value added per student for large private schools, based on the method described above. Value added is estimated to be 15.3 billion ID (0.013 billion USD).

Table 12.5 shows total value added by the services sector, which is estimated to be 1.99 trillion ID (1.72 billion USD).

Table 12.2
Value Added by Miscellaneous Services Sector Based on Survey (ID, billions)

Component	Erbil	Sulaymaniyah	Duhok
A: Value Added Estimated as Gross Output × Median Value Added to Output Ratio			
(1) Gross output	234.6	1,035.1	1,929.3
(2) Intermediate consumption	72.3	330.9	643.1
Median ratio (value added/ output) across classes	0.6916	0.6803	0.6666
(3) Gross value added	162.3	704.2	1,286.2
Overall total	2,152.7		
B: Value Added Adjusted for Firms with Top and Bottom 1 Percent of Output-to-Expenditure Ratio			
(1) Gross output	234.6	1,035.1	1,929.3
(2) Intermediate consumption	74.8	609.4	735.0
(3) Gross value added (1 – 2)	159.8	425.7	1,194.3
Overall total	1,779.8		
C: Average of Two Methods for Addressing Outliers			
(1) Gross output	234.6	1,035.1	1,929.3
(2) Intermediate consumption	73.6	470.1	689.0
(3) Gross value added (1 – 2)	161.1	565.0	1,240.2
Overall total	1,966.3		

Table 12.3
Value Added by Miscellaneous Services Sector Based on Survey, by Activity (ID, billions)

	Duhok		Sulaymaniyah		Erbil	
Activity	**Output**	**Value added**	**Output**	**Value added**	**Output**	**Value added**
Information and communications	14.9	10.6	66.5	38.5	13.3	7.9
Financial and insurance	10.5	7.7	291.3	134.2	68.5	28.5
Real estate	21.8	15.9	83.3	38.6	78.4	58.4
Professional, scientific, and technical	20.6	13.1	70.0	40.7	68.9	36.9
Human health and social work activities	7.7	5.8	50.5	36.5	105.6	77.6
Administrative and support services activities	40.3	30.0	114.7	79.6	1,406.5	908.0
Arts, entertainment, and recreation	35.5	21.8	51.9	36.0	86.9	60.1
Other service activities	83.3	56.2	306.9	160.9	101.2	62.8
Total	234.6	161.1	1,035.1	565.0	1,929.3	1,240.2

Table 12.4
Value Added by Private Hospitals, Different Methods (ID, billions)

Method	Value Added
Using value added per bed from Hospital #1	18.3
Using value added per bed from Hospital #2	17.8
Average	18.0

Table 12.5
Value Added by Miscellaneous Services Sector (ID, billions)

Category	Value Added
Services survey	1,966.3
Large private hospitals	18.0
Large private schools	15.3
Total	1,999.6

Discussion

In the case of the services survey, the list of firms was based on a 2009 sampling frame. It is likely that the number of services firms has risen since 2009, given overall growth in the KRI. Our calculations are thus likely to underestimate value added by this sector in 2012. At the same time, survey respondents typically provided information on costs and revenues from December 2013, and if per-firm value added has risen over time, our calculations may overestimate value added for 2012. On balance, we suspect it is more likely that the former effect dominates, and our calculations represent a lower bound on value added for this sector in 2012.

For large private hospitals and schools, a key assumption we made was that value added per bed or student could be extrapolated from the firms that were interviewed to other firms. In addition, in the case of schools, we assumed that the wages in the educational sector, reported in the Kurdistan Region Labor Force Survey, were a reasonable approximation of teacher salaries. In the future, value added estimates for these firms can be improved by directly collecting more detailed, up-to-date data.

CHAPTER THIRTEEN

Public Administration

This chapter presents estimates for value added for public administration.

Methods

Following standard practice in GDP accounting, we used an income approach to estimate the value added from public administration. We added up the value for compensation of employees and consumption of fixed capital, since net operating surplus was assumed to be zero.

Compensation of Employees

We received accounts that present aggregate expenditures of the government, as well as a breakdown into the following subcategories for 2012: salary of staff and retired, equipment and maintenance and services, subsidies, grants, social benefits, other expenses, and nonfinancial assets.

We used the subcategory "salary of staff and retired" to measure employee compensation. However, this subcategory included not only salaries but also pension payouts to retired employees. We also received a table documenting the value of pension payouts and pension contributions for current employees. We therefore subtracted the value of pension payouts (but not the value of pension contributions) from the "salary of staff and retired" to arrive at the estimated compensation for employees.

Consumption of Fixed Capital

There are three alternatives to estimate the consumption of fixed capital in the public sector. The first two consist of measuring the total fixed capital and estimating the depreciation rate to value its consumption. In the first method, total fixed capital and the depreciation rate are measured, directly, by conducting surveys of produced fixed assets at market prices during two consecutive periods and then calculating the decline in the market values of the stock of fixed assets. This can be a very expensive process, and it requires at least two years to implement; therefore, we did not use this method.

The second method is called the perpetual inventory method, and it is an indirect method recommended in the *System of National Accounts 2008*. This method involves an approximation of market valuation and is less costly to implement. It consists of estimating the investments made over a long period of time and aggregating these investments to estimate the total value of public sector fixed capital. However, this requires a long historical series of data on public investments, which is not available for the KRI.

The third and simplest method is to assume that the consumption of fixed capital equals a fixed proportion of the compensation of employees. This is currently the only feasible option for the KRI given the available data. In order to make a realistic assumption, we analyzed the ratio of consumption of fixed capital to value added for a variety of countries. This proportion ranges from close to zero to 36 percent.

Based on the countries that are at a similar stage of economic development to that of the KRI, we estimated the consumption of fixed capital is equal to 5 percent of the value added by government agencies.

Overlap with Government Services Estimated in Other Sectors

When estimating value added of various sectors in the KRI, our figures also included certain government services. This is true specifically for the banking sector, airports, and electricity. To avoid duplication, we subtracted salaries paid to government employees in government-owned banks and salaries paid to airport workers from our estimates of compensation to employees in public administration. However, the figure reported for salaries in the electricity sector appeared to be unrealistically high (200 billion ID or 172 million USD); therefore we did not subtract this amount.

Results

The value added to the KRI in 2012 was estimated to be 7.577 trillion ID (6.5 billion USD) (Table 13.1).

Table 13.1
Value Added by Public Administration (ID, billions)

Component	Value Added
Salary of staff and retired	7,965
Less: pensions	731
Less: bank salaries[a]	18.1
Less: airport salaries	17.5
Compensation of employees	7,198.4
Consumption of fixed capital estimate	378.9
Overall total (compensation of employees plus consumption of fixed capital)	7,577.3

[a] For bank salaries, we subtracted the salaries reported in the data on government expenditures received from the KRG, which is lower than the estimate based on salary data from the CSO on government-owned trade banks (48.5 billion ID, see Chapter Eleven). Similarly, for airport salaries, the amount reported in the data on government expenditures is lower than the estimate based on passenger flows (47.2 billion ID, see Chapter Eight). For consistency, we used the values reported in the data on government expenditures here; however, subtracting the estimates based on bank salary data and passenger flows would affect the overall total estimate of value added in Table 13.1 by less than 1 percent.

Discussion

The critical assumption used in our estimates of value added from public administration is the estimate of consumption of fixed capital. As discussed above, we estimated this percentage based on evidence from other countries. Once a longer time series of data are available for the KRI, a more accurate estimate can be made based on the perpetual inventory method or by directly measuring the depreciation rate.

We also note that we did not subtract salaries for the electricity sector from our estimates, because the reported values for electricity sector salaries appeared to be unrealistically high. In the future, the estimate of this component of the KRI's GRP would be improved by identifying more accurately the salaries associated with the electricity sector.

CHAPTER FOURTEEN

Home Ownership and Rental

This chapter presents estimates for value added that accrues to households from living in their homes each year. Typically, GRP estimates include value of "housing services" accruing to homeowners in addition to the rental income of those who rent property. The latter are explicit payments and are included in GRP, as this is income to the owners of the property (landlords) for housing services they provide. The housing services enjoyed by those who happen to be owners must be treated equivalently. In other words, services derived from dwellings in the year under consideration need to be part of GRP irrespective of whether the house is owned by the occupant. If they were not, GDP could be very different from one country to the next, or in the same country over time, simply because one country has relatively more rentals (counted) than home ownership (not counted).

Methods

Home Ownership

The approach to estimating the value of services from home ownership is to treat these services as equivalent to rent, and to estimate what the rent would be if the property were rented rather than owned.

We estimated the value of housing services accruing to homeowners based on the 2012 wave of the IHSES.[1] Specifically, we drew on data for households responding to the question "What is the ownership status of this dwelling?" with the answer "Owned by the household." We used these owners' self-reported rental values by taking the responses for the question, "If you were to reside in a similar dwelling, what would be the estimated rental monthly value?" We weighted the responses by the household weights given in the IHSES 2012 data. These

[1] Public use data for IHSES 2012 are available from CSO, 2012d.

monthly values were then multiplied by 12 to give annual gross output.[2] Intermediate consumption was assumed to be 20 percent.[3]

In an attempt to match the tabulated housing values reported in the official tabulations of IHSES 2012 as closely as possible, we obtained the code used by the CSO to create the tabulations. It appears that households that did not fully complete the survey were excluded, and certain household locations were re-categorized; we followed these examples. We also followed the CSO's code and dropped the proportion of imputed rent associated with running a household's business.

Home Rental

As discussed above, in many countries, rents are paid to businesses such as apartment owners and are thus automatically included as part of value added. However, our discussions with the KRSO indicate that most households in the KRI rent their homes from other individuals. Thus, the value added from rentals is unlikely to be captured elsewhere.

To account for rental value, we used the data from IHSES 2012 to analyze households who answered the question, "What is the ownership status of this dwelling?" with all answers *other than* "Owned by the household." We used each household's stated housing unit rent, on an annualized basis, weighted by the household weight given in the IHSES 2012 data.

Over half of the surveyed households that were not homeowners provided no value for the rent paid, as they would have been expected to given the survey structure. However, almost all of these households did answer the question, "If you were to reside in a similar dwelling, what would be the estimated rental monthly value?" It was not clear whether these households received free or subsidized rent, or whether the survey questions were misinterpreted. Given our understanding of the local context, we suspect it is the latter. Since our aim was to capture the total value of housing services, regardless of who pays for them, we used the imputed value of rent if paid rent was missing. As with owner-occupied housing, intermediate consumption was assumed to be 20 percent.

[2] We also applied an alternative method known as hedonic regression as a robustness check of our estimates of the value added from home ownership, also using data from IHSES 2012. This method involves conducting a regression analysis that shows how the annual rents reported by renters are related to a variety of housing characteristics, namely type of household (house, flat, mud homes, other), total area of dwelling, number of rooms, distance to road in kilometers, and interruption in the availability of water. The resulting regression coefficients can then be used to predict (impute) the rental value of housing for both renters and homeowners. We compared the values for both groups with the values reported in the survey. In the case of renters, the predicted values from the regression model were typically much higher (on the order of 100 percent higher) than the housing values that they reported. In the case of owners, the predicted housing values were fairly similar to the reported values (on average, 7 percent lower than the amount that owners reported that they would pay if they were renting). The large discrepancies between predicted and reported values for renters suggest that the linear hedonic regressions were not a good fit for the data. In particular, housing prices are largely determined by location, and we lacked highly specific location data. Therefore, we do not use the results of the hedonic regressions for our value added estimates and instead rely on reported potential rents.

[3] The 20 percent value is based on estimates from the United States as reported in Mayerhauser and Reinsdorf, 2007.

Results

The value added to the KRI in 2012 was estimated to be 1.793 trillion ID for home ownership (Table 14.1), and 563 billion ID for home rental (Table 14.2), for a total of 2.356 trillion ID (2.02 billion USD).

Discussion

Our estimates of value added from housing services rely on homeowners' estimates of what their rent would be if they were to rent their homes. While this method relies on homeowners' judgments and is thus potentially subject to bias (likely upward), it is in keeping with international practices for national income accounting.

Table 14.1
Value Added by Home Ownership (ID, billions)

Component	Erbil	Sulaymaniyah	Duhok
(1) Gross output	1,019	860	362
(2) Intermediate consumption	204	172	72
(3) Gross value added (1 – 2)	815	688	290
Overall total	1,793		

Table 14.2
Value Added by Home Rental (ID, billions)

Component	Erbil	Sulaymaniyah	Duhok
(1) Gross output	271	302	131
(2) Intermediate consumption	54	60	26
(3) Gross value added (1 – 2)	217	241	105
Overall total	563		

CHAPTER FIFTEEN

Conclusion and Recommendations

This report documents results from the first comprehensive calculation of GRP for the KRI, excluding the natural resources sector. A key benefit of the bottom-up approach taken in this report is the estimation of value added not just at the regional level, but for each main sector. Such statistics make it possible to characterize the importance of various sectors in the local economy and, in other words, the *structure* of the economy, when estimates are made in future years, to identify trends in sectoral growth.

Table 15.1 and Figure 15.1 summarize value added in each major sector in 2012. The largest nongovernment sectors, in terms of value added to the KRI in 2012, were construction (18.7 percent), wholesale and retail trade (9.1 percent), home ownership and rental (8.6 percent), and miscellaneous services (7.3 percent). The large contribution of construction to value added is consistent with the KRI's rapid economic growth. As elsewhere in the Middle East region, public administration plays a very large role in the economy, accounting for 27.6 percent of value added. It is important to note that the income approach used in the calculation of value added for this sector includes both value added generated by current operations and value added generated by internally undertaken investment expenditures. Also consistent with the region overall, the KRI's share of value added in agriculture is low (3.1 percent). This is the same as that reported by Jordan in 2012 (3.1 percent) and somewhat lower than that of Lebanon (6.1 percent) and Turkey (8.8 percent). Manufacturing contributed 6.1 percent of value added. This share is substantially lower than that reported by other countries in the region (19 percent for Jordan, 9 percent for Lebanon, 17 percent for Turkey), suggesting that there is room for expansion of this sector in the KRI as a source of future economic growth.[1]

As noted in Chapter One, to arrive at GRP, we need to add net taxes (taxes minus subsidies) to value added. Our discussions with staff at the KRSO and in the Ministry of Finance indicate that the KRI does not impose product taxes. We did note that, according to one document received from the KRSO, there may be product taxes imposed on money exchanges (see Table E.3). We do add them back in; however, the total sum is quite small (0.2 billion ID). As noted in Chapter Eleven, FISIM must be netted out in order to estimate total GRP. Since we lack information that would be required to allocate FISIM across industries and households, we follow *System of National Accounts 1993* guidance and treat all FISIM as if it were allocated to industries. As shown in Table 15.1, we estimate FISIM to be 58.4 billion ID, approximately 0.2 percent of value added. After adding net taxes and subtracting FISIM from value added, we arrive at a final GRP estimate of 27,381 billion ID (23.52 billion USD).

[1] Data for Jordan, Lebanon, and Turkey are from World Bank, 2015.

Table 15.1
Value Added, by Sector, in the Kurdistan Region—Iraq

Sector	ISIC Rev. 4 Code	Value Added (ID, billions)	Value Added (USD, billions)	Percentage of Total Value Added
Agriculture	A 01–03	840.1	0.72	3.1
Quarrying	B 05–09	42.5	0.037	0.2
Manufacturing	C 10–33	1,681.5	1.44	6.1
Electricity	D 35	555.9	0.48	2.0
Water	E 36–39	Included in public administration		
Construction	F 41–43	5,130.8	4.41	18.7
Wholesale and retail trade	G 45–47	2,499	2.15	9.1
Transportation and storage	H 49–53	1,752.9	1.51	6.4
Accommodation and food service	I 55–56	854.5	0.73	3.1
Information and communications (large firms)	J 58–63	1,844.3	1.58	6.7
Banking, insurance, money exchanges	K 64–66	305.3	0.26	1.1
Miscellaneous services	L, M, N, P, Q, R, S	1,999.6	1.72	7.3
Public administration	O 84	7,577.3	6.51	27.6
Home ownership and rental		2,355	2.02	8.6
Total value added		27,439	23.57	100.0
Plus: product taxes		0.223	0.0002	
Less: FISIM		58.4	0.0502	
Gross regional product		27,381	23.52	

Discussion and Recommendations

Given that this is the first comprehensive attempt to calculate GRP for the KRI, and one done under constraints of time, resources, and external circumstances beyond our control, our aim was to use available data as much as possible, keep new data collection to a minimum, and make reasonable assumptions to make the most out of the data in order to arrive at the best possible estimate. In many cases, we made a variety of assumptions to estimate value added from existing data, which were not necessarily collected for that purpose. In other cases, lack of existing data required the collection of new survey data to enable value added calculation. The specific challenges and limitations associated with each sector's value added calculations were detailed in Chapters Two through Fourteen.

Broadly speaking, the two main challenges associated with calculating GRP were as follows. First, the datasets or sampling frames used were sometimes from different time periods. The new surveys conducted for the miscellaneous services and transportation/storage sectors were based on a firm census from 2009. Given the growth in the region, it is highly likely that the number of firms in the population grew between 2009 and 2012, so our estimates will understate value added to some extent. Similarly, some of the existing datasets, such as

Figure 15.1
Value Added, by Sector, in the Kurdistan Region—Iraq

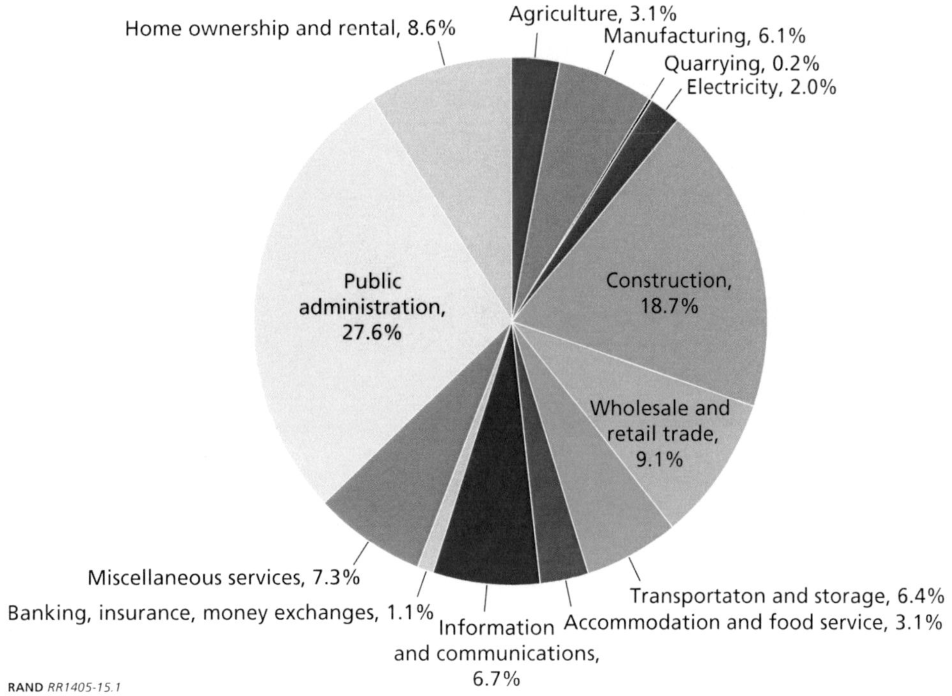

RAND *RR1405-15.1*

manufacturing and quarrying, were from years prior to 2012, so—assuming that value added per firm has grown over time—again it is likely that our estimates understate value added. In contrast, the construction, transportation and storage, and services surveys were conducted in the spring 2014 and reflect value added in that year. In these sectors, the underestimate of the number of firms may be offset by the overestimate associated with value added per firm.

Second, there are several sectors in which a few firms contribute a large share of value added. To ensure that these firms were not missed during sampling, KRSO staff conducted surveys of several hospitals, schools, and media firms, and we extrapolated value added estimates from those firms to estimate value added by all large firms in those sectors. We also collected publicly available information on large telecommunications firms, and we received information from the KRSO and the CSO on firms in the financial sector. Nonetheless, we were unable to obtain information on all large firms, so our estimates are based on extrapolations of value added for firms we were able to interview or from which we were able to gather information.

Finally, our calculations exclude the natural resources sector, because of lack of data availability. It is clearly important that future estimates include value added from this important sector. This will require data on revenues and costs from firms operating in this sector. These data could be collected at the firm level, using a survey akin to the manufacturing firm survey. Potential alternate data sources, should they be available in future, include administrative data on revenues and costs for this sector, as well as publicly available annual reports from large firms operating in the sector. It is important to note that not only production, but also allied activities such as exploration and processing, would need to be included in order to capture the full value added by this sector.

In the future, estimates of GRP would be improved by putting into place a set of streamlined and standardized procedures to gather the required information on value added from *all* sectors. The backbone of these procedures would be the implementation of an updated enterprise census. The best practice is to conduct an enterprise census every few ("benchmark") years. During interim years, it is advisable to count and gather limited information on revenues and employment from all large and medium firms, to ensure that the firms that account for the largest share of value added are fully represented. It would also be useful to collect more complete information from the small number of firms that are likely to contribute a large share of value added on an annual basis. A subset of firms may also be more fully surveyed in interim years. Putting into place such a system will also make it easier to update GRP for the KRI on an annual and systematic basis.

APPENDIX A

Agriculture

This appendix contains further details on the calculation of value added for the agriculture sector.

Data Cleaning and Adjustments

We cleaned the survey data and merged them with the census listings. Since the identifiers in the census did not correspond with those in the surveys, we merged the datasets using the farmer's name, village, subdistrict, district, and governorate. The resulting database contained all variables needed to calculate added value: expenses, yield, and area by crop at the farmer level within a geographic unit.

We had to make a variety of adjustments to the raw data, because there were a number of inconsistencies, including in the relationship between district names and codes and in the units in which prices were reported, as well as occasional miscaptured expenses, yields, and planted areas. For example, the yield for one farmer in Darbandykhan, Sulaymaniyah, was reported as 6,000,000 kilograms per donum; we divided this value by 1,000 to make it consistent with the observed yields for the same crop within that district. Table A.1 synthesizes the main challenges identified in the data.

Data Processing (Methodology)

To calculate value added, we first needed to inflate the data from the farmer-level survey to obtain results at the district and governorate levels. We used two methods for inflating the agricultural survey data. The first corresponds to the sampling strategy that was used for collecting the data: sample 10 percent of the villages in a subdistrict and two farmers in each village.

Using the sampling inflation method, we obtained the production of each governorate by applying the following formula:

$$Y_g = \sum_{d \in g} \left[\sum_{s \in d} \left\{ \sum_{v \in s} Y_{fv} * \left(\frac{F_v}{f_v} \right) \right\} * 10 \right]$$

where Y_{fv} is the total yield of surveyed farmers f in village v; F_v is the total number of farmers in the village v according to the census; f_v is the number of surveyed farmers in village v; the

Table A.1
Data Inconsistencies by Season and Governorate (2011/2012)

Season	Governorate	Errors Found
Winter	Duhok	• Expenses were captured in ID instead of thousands of ID. • The planted area from the survey diverged from the census. We used the area reported in the census.
	Erbil	• The planted area from the survey diverged from the census. We used the area reported in the census.
	Sulaymaniyah	• The planted area from the survey diverged from the census. We used the area reported in the census.
Summer	Duhok	• The planted area from the survey diverged from the census. We used the area reported in the census.
	Erbil	• Compared with the census, the surveyed planted area of a few farmers in Soran and Mergazor included additional zeros (e.g., 100 instead of 1). • Expenses and prices of a few farmers in three districts were systematically reported in ID instead of thousands of ID. • A few yields in six districts were miscaptured, including too many or too few zeros. We compared them with the distribution of yields for the same crop within each district and adjusted accordingly.
	Sulaymaniyah	• Expenses of a few farmers in three districts were reported in ID instead of thousands of ID. • One farmer in the district of Darbandykhan reported a yield of 6,000,000 kilograms per donum. We divided this value by 1,000. • When compared with the census, the surveyed planted area of few farmers in Darbandykhan included additional zeros. We used the planted area in the census. • In the report, data for district Mawat was included in district Nawandy Sulaymaniyah.

SOURCE: Authors' observations based on the 2011/2012 farm-level agriculture survey and the 2011/2012 agriculture census listings.

innermost summation is over all the villages in the subdistrict s; the intermediate summation is over all the subdistricts in district d; and the outermost summation is over all the districts in governorate g, to give the total production of governorate Y_g.

We then used the inflation factors to check whether the estimated production was reasonable. To do so, we inflated the land under cultivation and checked it against the values reported in the census. The former was quite a bit higher (on average, ten times higher). Therefore, we applied a second method for inflating the survey data. This method used the land under cultivation reported in the survey and the land under cultivation in the district reported in the census to calculate the inflation factors. By construction, this means that the amount of (inflated) land estimated from the survey will match the amount of land reported in the census.

Using the land inflation method, we obtained the production of each governorate by applying the following formula:

$$Y_g = \sum_{d \in g} Y_{fd} * \left(\frac{L_d}{l_d} \right)$$

where Y_{fd} is the total yield of surveyed farmers f in district d; L_d is the total planted area in the district according to the census; l_d is the total planted land from the surveys in district d; and Y_g is the total production of governorate g. One could alternatively inflate successively by land represented by the surveyed farmers in the village, the land represented by the villages in the subdistrict, and so on; however, this would reduce to the formula above, since we are ignoring the sampling scheme in this method.

Since the inflation factors for these methods are very different, they result in very different GRP calculations. Tables A.2 and A.3 show estimated value added for Duhok using the two different methods.

The first approach results in larger production but an overestimate of land relative to the census; the second results in less production but an exact calculation of land. We compared our results to those reported by the Ministry of Agriculture (Kurdistan Region—Iraq Ministry of Agriculture, 2012). We were able to verify that the reported numbers were close to what we calculated based on the second method, and we chose to follow this method.

Table A.2
Value Added by Agriculture in Duhok Using Inflation Method 1 (Sampling Methodology)

District Name	Average Inflation Factor, by Farmer	Land from Survey	Total Value (B)	Total Cultivating Expenses (C)	Added Value (B – C)
Duhok Center	6.4	34,575	17,627,492	2,351,500	15,275,992
Sumel	5.3	253,550	91,011,235	28,002,174	63,009,061
Zakho	2.4	110,060	72,115,646	14,506,796	57,608,850
Amadia	7.1	22,150	22,380,701	3,877,596	18,503,105
Shekhan	15	141,450	29,156,596	17,174,141	11,982,455
Akra	18.5	144,490	74,931,733	12,993,788	61,937,945
Bardarash	21.9	283,375	63,644,035	27,610,349	36,033,686
Total	12	989,650	370,867,439	106,516,346	264,351,093

Table A.3
Value Added by Agriculture in Duhok Using Inflation Method 2 (Inflating Based on Reported Land)

District Name	Average Inflation Factor, by Land	Land from Census	Total Value (B)	Total Cultivating Expenses (C)	Added Value (B – C)
Duhok Center	23.3	19,997	12,423,704	1,487,330	10,936,374
Sumel	25.4	174,001	57,438,595	17,785,610	39,652,985
Zakho	16.8	76,066	47,501,656	9,556,044	37,945,612
Amadia	13.1	6,998	8,243,820	1,436,885	6,806,935
Shekhan	103.5	176,998	33,478,312	20,534,677	12,943,635
Akra	93.1	91,393	52,392,487	8,466,521	43,925,966
Bardarash	86	165,696	36,842,047	16,124,019	20,718,028
Total	59.8	711,148	248,320,620	75,391,085	172,929,535

Data processing also included the imputation of missing data. Some districts and governorates reported planted area in the census listing but their corresponding yields were missing in the agriculture survey. For instance, according to the census listing, the five types of winter crops (listed in Table 2.1) were planted in all three governorates; however, in the data from the surveys, there was no information for lentils or vegetables for Duhok and Erbil, and only information for chickpeas in few districts. Similar cases were found in the summer survey data.

We decided to impute the yield per donum in the areas where the census reported that that those types of crops were planted. We imputed yield based on the average yield of the same type of crop at the lowest level of aggregation available. For example, if one of the farmers in a village had missing data on yield, we used the other farmer's yield; if a subdistrict had missing data, we used average yield information from other subdistricts in that district; and so on. If survey data were completely missing for a governorate, we imputed data from the other governorates. For the missing survey data on lentils and vegetables for Duhok and Erbil, we applied the average yield per donum from Sulaymaniyah for each of these crops to the entire governorate and then multiplied them by the planted area for that governorate reported in the census. We did not adjust for the differences in the fertility of land between governorates or districts.

Finally, we did not have prices of winter crops from farmers. We calculated the winter GRP using CPI data provided by the KRSO. Prices were for Hawler Center in January 2012. Prices for summer crops were provided by the KRSO. Table A.4 reports the final prices used.

Table A.4
Price (ID) per Kilogram of Production, by Crop and Season

Summer				Winter	
Product	Sulaymaniyah	Duhok	Erbil	Product	All Governorates
Rice	2,600	3,000	1,500	Wheat	1,500
Sunflower	1,250	1,900	1,100	Barley	1,500
Sesame	2,000	3,750	2,250	Chickpeas	2,875
Grasspeas	1,250	2,750	1,450	Lentils	2,375
Potatoes	550	550	300	Vegetables	1,481
Corn	450	450			
Tobacco	5,000	12,000			
Fsteqa Arabi	1,813	1,813			
Tomatoes	750	600	550		
Okra	1,350	2,000	2,100		
Eggplant	750	600	600		
Cucumbers	600	560	700		
String Beans	1,250	1,350	1,600		
Beans	1,700	1,200	1,800		
Squash	500	600	570		
Watermelon	450	400	400		
Armenian Cucumbers	600	700	600		
Melon	450	450	400		
Green peppers	800	800	750		
Onions	700	800	800		
Cotton	1,800	1,800	1,800		

SOURCE: Summer prices from the KRSO. Winter prices calculated by authors based on CPI data from the KRSO.

Tables A.5 through A.10 provide a detailed breakdown of value added by governorate and season.

Table A.5
Winter Agriculture Value Added in Duhok

District Name	Total Value (thousand ID) (A)	Total Cultivating Expenses (thousand ID) (B)	Added Value (thousand ID) (A – B)	Production (tons)	Planted Land (donums)
Duhok Center	12,423,704	1,487,330	10,936,374	7,897	25,330
Sumel	57,438,595	17,785,610	39,652,985	38,208	182,280
Zakho	47,501,656	9,556,044	37,945,612	31,403	78,426
Amadia	8,243,820	1,436,885	6,806,935	5,290	11,638
Shekhan	33,478,312	20,534,677	12,943,635	21,312	186,962
Akra	52,392,487	8,466,521	43,925,966	33,363	104,899
Bardarash	36,842,047	16,124,019	20,718,027	23,932	192,677
Total	248,320,620	75,391,085	172,929,535	161,406	782,219

Table A.6
Winter Agriculture Value Added in Sulaymaniyah

District Name	Total Value (thousand ID) (A)	Total Cultivating Expenses (thousand ID) (B)	Added Value (thousand ID) (A – B)	Production (tons)	Planted Land (donums)
Pshdar	19,540,563	6,865,474	12,675,090	12,546	58,523
Penjween	6,215,270	2,900,502	3,314,767	4,057	17,794
Kanaqen	37,603,453	8,804,181	28,799,272	25,034	109,482
Darbandikhan	8,643,714	2,096,106	6,547,608	5,710	23,548
Dokan	60,542,012	14,543,532	45,998,480	39,011	126,982
Rania	20,421,771	5,434,472	14,987,299	13,540	52,548
Said Sadik	41,324,353	14,794,975	26,529,378	27,498	73,683
Sharbazher	5,178,010	947,080	4,230,930	3,229	7,816
Sharazoor	31,545,624	9,173,314	22,372,310	21,010	49,480
Chamchamal	27,072,953	13,059,659	14,013,294	17,963	192,356
Qaradaqh	13,606,577	2,672,699	10,933,878	9,029	19,834
Kalar	23,811,668	3,805,468	20,006,200	15,807	68,824
Kfri	21,054,191	4,604,958	16,449,233	14,036	84,834
Mawat	2,469,061	423,928	2,045,133	1,501	3,928
Sulaimany center	52,208,588	13,762,308	38,446,280	34,629	113,061
Halabja	29,184,324	12,738,749	16,445,575	19,340	73,596
Total	400,422,132	116,627,403	283,794,729	263,942	1,080,012

Table A.7
Winter Agriculture Value Added in Erbil

District Name	Total Value (thousand ID) (A)	Total Cultivating Expenses (thousand ID) (B)	Added Value (thousand ID) (A – B)	Production (tons)	Planted Land (donums)
Erbil Center	46,155,719	16,518,695	29,637,024	30,767	172,404
Erbil Dasht	47,468,575	14,255,224	33,213,351	31,556	179,830
Soran	8,853,760	3,305,108	5,548,652	5,819	16,170
Shaqlawa	32,796,730	12,063,925	20,732,805	20,915	143,857
Choman	2,188,616	780,962	1,407,653	1,453	4,282
Koya	34,183,577	12,873,297	21,310,279	22,684	115,437
Mergasor	3,694,728	1,934,245	1,760,483	2,458	7,150
Khabat	30,348,663	7,719,075	22,629,588	20,189	107,536
Rawandoz	2,194,571	847,791	1,346,779	1,434	4,603
Total	207,884,938	70,298,324	137,586,614	137,275	751,268

Table A.8
Summer Agriculture Value Added in Duhok

District Name	Total Value (thousand ID) (A)	Total Cultivating Expenses (thousand ID) (B)	Added Value (thousand ID) (A – B)	Total Production (tons)	Planted Land (donums)
Duhok Center	5,591,092	2,098,904	3,492,188	9,742	4,428
Sumel	9,781,200	2,039,669	7,741,531	16,268	2,242
Zakho	1,313,450	711,455	601,995	2,760	3,269
Amadia	17,665,720	1,759,399	15,906,321	29,557	2,978
Shekhan	30,356,346	9,519,640	20,836,706	54,471	22,254
Akra	24,312,080	5,815,997	18,496,083	36,607	20,415
Bardarash	27,555,570	9,855,908	17,699,662	38,677	23,726
Total	116,575,458	31,800,971	84,774,487	188,083	79,312

Table A.9
Summer Agriculture Value Added in Sulaymaniyah

District Name	Total Value (thousand ID) (A)	Total Cultivating Expenses (thousand ID) (B)	Added Value (thousand ID) (A – B)	Total Production (tons)	Planted Land (donums)
Sharbazher	6,310,750	2,229,737	4,081,013	9,908	3,536
Khanaqin	2,304,550	529,927	1,774,623	2,484	791
Darbandykhan	2,598,350	296,655	2,301,695	4,085	1,859
Dukan	6,445,370	2,022,764	4,422,606	10,913	8,093
Ranya	534,318	140,463	393,855	682	587
Saydsadq	4,783,292	845,579	3,937,713	9,008	3,226
Chamchamal	1,681,950	739,941	942,009	2,531	1,646
Mawat	2,675,400	1,999,741	675,659	3,194	1,970
Sharazwr	3,395,100	150,486	3,244,614	6,036	2,170
Qaradaqh	395,645	135,921	259,724	448	135
Pshdar	3,975,400	1,061,457	2,913,943	5,039	2,900
Penjwen	26,269,650	8,174,590	18,095,060	40,090	7,730
Kalar	695,931	309,090	386,841	1,068	437
Kfry	200,300	158,567	41,733	159	127
Nawandy Slemany	11,713,533	2,622,233	9,091,300	21,876	14,541
Halabja	1,817,354	706,638	1,110,716	3,461	3,226
Total	75,796,893	22,123,789	53,673,104	120,982	52,970

Table A.10
Summer Agriculture Value Added in Erbil

District Name	Total Value (thousand ID) (A)	Total Cultivating Expenses (thousand ID) (B)	Added Value (thousand ID) (A – B)	Total Production (tons)	Planted Land (donums)
Khabat	28,641,330	7,046,588	21,594,742	51,710	7,349
Dashte Hawler	7,647,610	3,939,381	3,708,229	15,104	6,429
Rawandoz	3,305,091	881,435	2,423,656	4,256	854
Soran	12,600,500	2,810,372	9,790,128	22,243	3,920
Shaqlawa	4,392,890	1,881,029	2,511,861	8,759	6,540
Choman	48,557,360	37,720,113	10,837,247	78,319	10,717
Koya	7,560,055	2,236,361	5,323,694	11,393	6,049
Mergasor	3,660,540	2,243,036	1,417,504	7,226	1,492
Nawande Hawler	66,111,010	16,401,762	49,709,248	114,758	17,431
Total	182,476,386	75,160,077	107,316,309	313,767	60,782

APPENDIX B

Manufacturing

This appendix provides details on the specific components used to estimate gross output and intermediate consumption for large and medium firms, as well as estimates of value added, by two-digit ISIC Revision 3 code.

Gross Output of Large and Medium Manufacturing Firms

Table B.1 shows the survey items that we used to measure each component of gross output. Below, we provide further details of how we treated each survey item.

Value of shipments/turnover/sales of goods or services produced. We began by adding up the value of net sales as reported in the survey. Eighty-three out of 89 large firms and 223 of out 236 medium firms reported domestic or export net sales. We assumed that "net sales" referred to the prices actually received by the producer, and thus already excluded any product taxes

Table B.1
Methods for Calculating Components of Gross Output

Component of Gross Output	Large and Medium Firms
Value of shipments/turnover/sales of goods or services produced	Net sales listed in product table
Value of sale/turnover/shipments of all goods and services purchased for resale in the same condition as received	Net sales of goods purchased for the purpose of sale + commission received + miscellaneous revenues (sale of containers and forms)
Purchases of goods and services for resale in the same condition as received	Goods purchased for the purpose of sale (domestic plus imports)
Receipts for industrial work done or industrial services rendered to others	Revenues from service activities + revenues from operations for the benefit of others
Other revenues	Rents from fixed assets (excluding land)
Value of own-account fixed assets	Change in inventory of "Cost of internally manufactured assets" (not included due to data discrepancies)
Change in work-in-progress	Change in inventory value of unfinished good inventories (as physical quantities were not available, this was calculated as the change in value)
Change in inventories of finished goods	Change in value of finished good inventories (as physical quantities were available, this was calculated as change in physical quantity multiplied by average price)
Change in inventories of goods purchased for resale in the same condition as received	Change in value of goods for the purpose of sale inventories (as physical quantities were not available, this was calculated as the change in value)

and included product subsidies (although our discussions with the KRSO and the Ministry of Finance suggest that product taxes are uncommon in the KRI).

Value of sale/turnover/shipments of all goods and services purchased for resale in the same condition as received. We added up the value of all "commercial activity expenses," including net sales of goods for the purpose of sale, commissions received, and miscellaneous revenues from the sale of containers and forms. Only four large firms and four medium firms reported positive values.

Purchases of goods and services for resale in the same condition as received. Two large firms and six medium firms reported this item. These were subtracted from the above revenues for sales.

Receipts for industrial work done or industrial services rendered to others. We added up all revenues from service activities plus "revenues from operations for the benefit of others." Only eight large firms reported and 13 medium firms provided services under this category.

Other revenues. No large or medium firms reported receiving rent from fixed assets (excluding land).

Value of own-account fixed assets. Four large firms reported a cost of internally manufactured assets, but the data appear incomplete. In three of the four cases, only beginning inventories were reported; in the fourth case, the beginning and ending inventories were the same. For medium firms, four reported a beginning value, but only two reported an ending value. Also, this item does not appear to be separately identified in two tables that contain details on assets; therefore we excluded this item from gross output calculations.

Change in work-in-progress. We used the change in the inventory of unfinished products. Opening and closing values of these inventories were only reported in terms of value (not quantity), so we used the change in inventory value to measure value added. Two large firms and one medium-sized firm reported beginning and ending inventories in this category.

Change in inventories of finished goods. To value changes in inventories of finished goods, we multiplied the change in stock (closing minus opening) by the average price. This method avoided including any holding gains or other revaluation of inventory in value added. Thirteen large firms and 82 medium-sized firms reported changes in inventories of finished goods.

Change in inventories of goods purchased for resale in the same condition as received. Opening and closing values of these inventories were only reported in terms of value (not quantity), so we used the change in inventory value to measure value added. No large firms and just one medium-sized firm reported beginning or ending inventories of this item.

Intermediate Consumption of Large and Medium-Sized Manufacturing Firms

Table B.2 shows the survey items that we used to measure each component of intermediate consumption. Below, we provide further details of how we treated each survey item.

Cost of raw materials and supplies. We began by adding up the cost of domestic and imported raw materials and packing materials as reported in the survey, less the value of materials sold without processing. Seventy-nine out of 83 large firms and 220 out of 236 medium-sized firms reported purchases of raw materials. Forty out of 83 large firms and 68 out of 236 medium-sized firms reported purchases of packing materials. We also added the cost of provisional tools, supplies and equipment, stationery, and workers' equipment, less the value sold without processing. Seventy-eight out of 83 large firms and 220 out of 236 medium-sized firms reported purchases of tools or other equipment. No large firms and one medium-sized firm reported raw materials, packing materials, or other equipment used without processing.

Table B.2
Methods for Calculating Components of Intermediate Consumption

Component of Intermediate Consumption	Large and Medium Firms
Cost of raw materials and supplies except gas, fuels, and electricity	Value of raw materials purchased during the year – value of raw materials sold without processing + value of packing materials purchased during the year – value of packing materials sold without processing + value of tools, supplies, etc., purchased during the year – value of tools, supplies, etc., sold without processing
Cost of gas, fuel, and electricity purchased	Value of refined oil products purchased – value of refined oil products sold without processing + value of liquid gas purchased – value of liquid gas sold without processing + value of lubricants and greases purchased – value of lubricants sold without processing + value of natural gas purchased – value of natural gas sold without processing + value of electricity purchased – value of electricity sold without processing
Cost of water and sewerage services	Value of water purchased – value of water sold without processing
Purchases of services except rental	Service needs (maintenance and miscellaneous)
Rental payments	Rents for fixed assets (excluding land)
Changes in inventories of materials, fuels, and supplies	Changes in inventory of raw materials, fuel and oil, electricity, water, packing materials, tools, supplies, and workers' equipment

Cost of gas, fuel, and electricity purchased. We added up the reported values of refined oil products, liquid gas, lubricants and greases, natural gas, and electricity purchased (domestic and imported), less the value sold without processing. All but one large and one medium-sized firm reported some type of cost of fuel or electricity. No large or medium-sized firms reported fuel or electricity sold without processing.

Cost of water and sewerage services. We added up the reported values of water purchased, less the value sold without processing, reported by 29 large firms and 59 medium-sized firms.

Purchases of services except rental. We added up all purchased services reported in the survey including maintenance, travel, and other services. All but two large firms and three medium-sized firms reported service payments of some type.

Rental payments. We added up rental payments for fixed assets (including buildings and facilities, tools and equipment, transportation, kits and molds, and office furniture, but excluding land). Forty-five large firms and 81 medium-sized firms reported paying rent for fixed assets.

Changes in inventories of materials, fuels, and supplies. We calculated the changes in inventories of raw materials (reported by 35 large and 106 medium-sized firms), packing materials (reported by 18 large and 16 medium-sized firms), fuels (reported by 20 large and 68 medium-sized firms), and supplies (reported by 24 large and 71 medium-sized firms). All inventories were valued by multiplying the change in stock by the average price.

Table B.3 presents estimates of gross output and intermediate consumption for large, medium-sized, and small firms, by two-digit ISIC Revision 3 code.

Table B.3
Gross Output and Intermediate Consumption by Manufacturing Firms, by Industry and Firm Size (ID, billions)

ISIC Revision 3 Code	Industry Name	Large		Medium		Small	
		Gross Output	Intermediate Consumption	Gross Output	Intermediate Consumption	Gross Output	Intermediate Consumption
15	Food	230	139	81	43	261	146
17	Textiles	45	25	0.2	0.05	3	2
18	Wearing Apparel	–	–	–	–	102	30
19	Leather	–	–	9	2	–	–
20	Wood	–	–	1	1	146	60
21	Paper	4	1	58	23	–	–
22	Printing	8	2	1	1	20	7
23	Coke, Petroleum and Nuclear Fuel	38	29	2	1	–	–
24	Rubber	31	25	2	2	–	–
25	Products Made of Oil and Coal	19	15	7	5	75	48
26	Non-Metal Mineral Products	935	395	197	100	262	182
27	Basic Metals	182	74	3	2	–	–
28	Fabricated Metal Products	24	14	20	10	340	153
29	Machinery	12	9	10	5	–	–
31	Electrical Machinery	34	24	1	0.3	–	–
36	Miscellaneous	17	9	6	2	131	50
	Total	1,580	762	397	196	1,341	678

APPENDIX C

Electricity

This appendix presents detailed calculations for value added from MoE (Table C.1) and large generators (Table C.2).

Table C.1
Value Added by the Ministry of Electricity (ID, billions)

Department	(1) Staff expenses	(2) Goods and services	(3) Subsidies	(4) Social benefits	(5) Other expenses	(6) Non-financial assets	(7) Total	Value added = (7) – (2)
Dewan	5.70	731.47	1.85	0.18	0.01	0.13	739.33	7.86
Erbil	44.49	13.61	–	0.22	0.35	17.37	76.04	62.43
Selmani	94.26	10.10	–	0.13	10.93	15.69	131.11	121.02
Duhok	18.24	21.26	–	0.06	8.02	1.03	48.61	27.35
Police	37.12	0.80	–	0.02	–	0.36	38.30	37.51
Total	199.81	777.24	1.85	0.61	19.32	34.59	1,033.40	256.16

Table C.2
Value Added by Large Electricity Generators (ID, billions)

Name of Generator	Output	Value Added (assumed 40% of output)
1000 MW Erbil	205.6	82.2
1000 MW Chamchamal	203.5	81.4
500 MW Duhok	114.2	45.7
150 MW Bahadra	38.2	15.3
Medial East power company 29 MW	4.4	1.7
Bander power company 29 MW	0.7	0.3
Medial West power company Duhok 29 MW	0.2	0.1
Total	566.82	226.73

APPENDIX D

Wholesale and Retail Trade

Table D.1 shows the survey items that we used to measure each component of gross output. Below, we provide further details of how we treated each survey item.

Value of sale/turnover/shipments of all goods and services purchased for resale in the same condition as received. We began by adding up the value of sales as reported in the survey. Net sales were reported by 789 out of 968 Erbil firms, 934 out of 1,071 Sulaymaniyah firms, and 499 out of 564 Duhok firms. We assumed that "sales" referred to the prices actually received by the producer (i.e., net sales), and thus already excluded any product taxes but included any product subsidies.

Purchases of goods and services for resale in the same condition as received. We included the value of purchases of goods purchased for resale. Values were reported by 774 Erbil firms, 932 Sulaymaniyah firms, and 489 Duhok firms.

Other revenues. This category includes revenues collected from the sale of products from established production, revenues from transport and forwarding services provided to others, revenues from the rental of machinery and equipment and transport, revenues for the provision of maintenance services, commissions for the sale of products and goods for others, and revenues from the rental of buildings. Other revenues were reported by 186 out of 968 Erbil firms, 260 out of 1,071 Sulaymaniyah firms, and 136 out of 564 Duhok firms.

Table D.1
Methods for Calculating Components of Gross Output

Component of Gross Output	Trade Firms
Value of sale/turnover/shipments of all goods and services purchased for resale in the same condition as received	Sales
Purchases of goods and services for resale in the same condition as received	Value of purchases of goods purchased for resale
Other revenues	Revenues from the sale of products from established production + revenues from transport and forwarding services provided to others + revenues from the rental of machinery and equipment and transport + revenues for the provision of maintenance services + commissions for the sale of products and goods for others + revenues from the rental of buildings
Change in inventories of goods purchased for resale in the same condition as received	Closing stock of goods purchased for resale opening stock of goods purchased for resale

Change in inventories of goods purchased for resale in the same condition as received. We subtracted the opening value from the closing value of goods purchased for resale to get the change in inventory value.

Table D.2 shows the survey items that we used to measure each component of intermediate consumption. Below, we provide further details of how we treated each survey item.

Cost of raw materials and supplies. We summed the reported values of raw materials, inventories of tools, packaging materials, and other goods (cleaning products, etc.) reported in the survey. From all governorates, 66 out of 2,603 firms reported raw materials, 63 firms reported inventories of tools, 1,580 firms reported packaging materials, and 1,521 firms reported other goods.

Cost of gas, fuel, and electricity purchased. We added up the reported values of fuel and fuel oils and the value of electricity purchased. 438 out of 968 Erbil firms, 352 out of 1,071 Sulaymaniyah firms, and 136 out of 564 Duhok firms reported fuel and fuel oils, while 837 out of 968 Erbil firms, 1,017 out of 1,071 Sulaymaniyah firms, and 532 out of 564 Duhok firms reported electricity purchases.

Cost of water and sewerage services. We added up the reported values of water purchased, reported by 362 Erbil firms, 344 Sulaymaniyah firms, and 229 Duhok firms.

Purchases of services except rental. We added up all service purchases reported in the survey including maintenance, shipping, and other services. All but 111 firms reported service payments of some type.

Rental payments. We included the rental payments for buildings. 643 Erbil firms, 823 Sulaymaniyah firms, and 437 Duhok firms reported paying rent.

Table D.3 presents estimates of gross output, intermediate consumption, and value added for trade firms by governorate, by three-digit ISIC Revision 4 code.

Table D.2
Methods for Calculating Components of Intermediate Consumption

Component of Intermediate Consumption	Trade Firms
Cost of raw materials and supplies except gas, fuels, and electricity	Cost of raw materials + cost of reserves tools + cost of packaging materials + cost of other goods (cleaning materials, etc.)
Cost of gas, fuel and electricity purchased	Cost of fuel and fuel oils + cost of electricity
Cost of water and sewerage services	Cost of water
Purchases of services except rental	Cost of post, telegraph and communications + cost of maintenance and repair (fixed assets) + shipping expenses + expenses for loading, unloading, transporting goods + accountants and lawyers fees + advertising and promotion expenses + cost of other services (cleaning services, etc.)
Rental payments	Rents for buildings

Table D.3
Gross Output and Intermediate Consumption by Trade Firms, by Industry and Governorate (ID, billions)

ISIC Revision 4 Code	Industry Name	Erbil		Sulaymaniyah		Duhok	
		Gross Output	Intermediate Consumption	Gross Output	Intermediate Consumption	Gross Output	Intermediate Consumption
451	Sale of Motor Vehicles	232	169	281	267	7	3
452	Maintenance and Repair of Motor Vehicles	152	81	99	15	160	127
453	Sale of Motor Vehicle Parts and Accessories	252	212	219	185	86	71
454	Sale, Maintenance and Repair of Motorcycles and Related Parts and Accessories	2	1	7	6	0	0
461	Wholesale on a Fee or Contract Basis	26	9	255	225	61	35
462	Wholesale of Agricultural Raw Materials and Live Animals	40	35	173	161	40	33
463	Wholesale of Food, Beverages and Tobacco	360	338	219	202	696	629
464	Wholesale of Household Goods	206	172	251	222	696	678
465	Wholesale of Machinery, Equipment and Supplies	23	20	57	51	15	11
466	Other Specialized Wholesale	2,015	1,941	530	472	444	409
469	Non-Specialized Wholesale Trade	46	45	15	13	3	2
471	Retail Sale in Non-Specialized Stores	725	565	561	475	496	424
472	Retail Sale of Food, Beverages and Tobacco in Specialized Stores	747	650	854	727	474	403
473	Retail Sale of Automotive Fuel in Specialized Stores	267	215	392	361	360	347
474	Retail Sale of Information and Communications Equipment in Specialized Stores	192	169	326	297	105	93
475	Retail Sale of Other Household Equipment in Specialized Stores	3,162	2,953	836	719	488	425
476	Retail Sale of Cultural and Recreation Goods in Specialized Stores	53	43	104	86	24	19
477	Retail Sale of Other Goods in Specialized Stores	1,747	1,468	738	609	576	525
478	Retail Sale via Stalls and Markets	20	15	13	11	38	31
479	Retail Trade Not in Stores, Stalls or Markets	1	0	1	1	26	26
	Total	10,269	9,104	5,932	5,104	4,798	4,291

APPENDIX E

Banking, Insurance, and Money Exchanges

Tables E.1 and E.2 provide detailed estimates of value added by local and Iraqi private banks, respectively. Table E.3 provides detailed estimates of value added by money exchanges, and Table E.4 shows calculations for FISIM.

Table E.1
Value Added by Local Private Banks (ID, billions)

Bank	2012 Total Value Added Estimation	2012 Value Added Attributed to the KRI	Source and Method
Kurdistan International Bank	48.1	44.0	Source: 2012 Annual Reports, Methods: Income approach, share of KRI branches in profits
Cihan Bank	42.5	32.5	Source: 2012 Annual Reports, Methods: Income approach, share of KRI branches in profits
Erbil Bank	31.0	26.0	2011 CSO estimation. 2012 growth and allocation of activity to the KRI as average of two other local banks
Total	121.6	102.5	

Table E.2
Value Added by Private Iraqi Banks Operating in the Kurdistan Region—Iraq (ID, billions)

Estimation Method	Value
Total 2011 value added of 21 banks, using CSO file	413.9
Estimating 2012 value added using Iraq Banking and Insurance GDP annual nominal growth rate (30.4 percent)	539.8
Attribution of 21.5 percent to the KRI	**116.1**

Table E.3
Value Added by Money Exchanges Operating in the Kurdistan Region—Iraq (ID, thousands)

Province	Output[a]	Intermediate Consumption[b]	Taxes and Fees[c]	Compensation of Employees	Total Operating Surplus	Total Value Added at Producer Prices	Total Value Added at Basic Prices
Duhok	6,837,494	934,672	94,589	995,810	4,812,423	5,902,822	5,808,233
Sulaymaniyah	10,941,998	1,398,817	75,986	2,707,010	6,760,185	9,543,181	9,467,195
Erbil	4,975,347	664,709	52,290	819,850	3,438,498	4,310,638	4,258,348
Total	22,754,839	2,998,198	222,865	4,522,670	15,011,106	19,756,641	19,533,776

SOURCE: KRSO table titled "Table (13): output value and the total value added by the provinces (value in thousand dinars)."

[a] Literally translated as "The total value of production."

[b] Literally translated as "The total value of goods and services."

[c] We assume these are taxes on products, since they equal the difference between gross value added in producer prices and gross value added in basic prices.

As noted in Chapter Eleven, we estimated FISIM by subtracting total interest paid from total interest received by banking institutions. Unfortunately, we do not observe explicit service charges, or a breakdown of loans and deposits by industries versus households. Thus, we follow *System of National Accounts 1993* guidance and treat all FISIM as if it were allocated to industries. Data we received from the CSO enabled this calculation for 2011 for local KRI private banks, Iraqi private banks, and foreign banks. The required data on interest were not available for government-owned trade banks.

We allocated the share of Iraqi-wide FISIM to the KRI in a similar manner as we allocated value added in the banking sector to the KRI (see Chapter Eleven) based the same data file from the CSO.

The 2011 figures were inflated to 2012 by the same growth rate of FISIM that was observed in Iraqi national accounts between 2012 and 2011 (5.66 percent). In the absence of more-detailed data, we assume that all FISIM is allocated to industries and government.

Table E.4
Financial Intermediation Services Indirectly Measured (ID, billions)

Category	Amount
Total FISIM of banks	58.4
Local private banks	17.7
Iraqi private banks	39.6
Foreign banks	1.1

APPENDIX F

Sampling and Design of New Surveys

We describe here the sampling methodology used for the miscellaneous services and transport/storage services surveys described in Chapter Twelve and also outline the structure of the questionnaires for these surveys. Appendix G, in a separate online document, presents the full questionnaires in English for other (miscellaneous) services as well as for construction (described in Chapter Six).

Sampling Design and Sample Size for Transportation/Storage and Miscellaneous Services Surveys

The 2009 census allowed us to identify firms based on their ISIC Revision 4 activity codes, permitting us to select for each survey a random sample of enterprises in the sectors in which we were interested and to stratify the sample based on these divisions. We followed the general approach to sampling used in other enterprise surveys carried out by the CSO and the KRSO. We stratified on activity and governorate, meaning that each activity in each governorate was a stratum from which a separate sample was randomly drawn. Compared with a simple random sample, which draws from the entire population of interest (all firms in these activities in all governorates), stratification ensures that all strata are represented in the survey.

For the services survey, the activities are the following, as already noted in Chapter Twelve:

1. Information and Communications
2. Finance and Insurance
3. Real Estate
4. Professional, Scientific and Technical Activities
5. Human Health and Social Work Activities
6. Administrative and Support Services Activities
7. Arts, Entertainment and Recreation
8. Other Service Activities.

With eight activities and three governorates, we have a total of 24 strata for the services survey. For the transportation and storage survey, we simply stratify on all transportation and all storage activities. Therefore there are six strata (two activities times three governorates).

Another benefit of stratification by activity (and by area) is that it gives us the opportunity to adjust the sample size in strata for which we want more precise or accurate estimates, that is, estimates of value added that have a small margin of error. The sample size in those strata can be adjusted (increased) to ensure this outcome. For our purposes, it was desirable to have reasonable precision both for transportation/storage overall and for combined other services. Since other services and transportation/storage are separate surveys, this amounts to choosing adequate sample sizes for each survey to ensure reasonable precision for mean value added for each survey. We note that there was little reason to choose sample sizes for individual smaller activities to ensure a low margin of error for these as well, and this would also have come at the cost of needing a much larger overall sample. Therefore, we did not oversample smaller strata (or, conversely, undersample larger ones). The sampling is thus one of proportional stratification.

We (1) stratified the sample on each of the activities above (and on governorate) to ensure a representative sample and (2) selected sample sizes for transportation/storage and for other services to ensure that we would be able to make reasonably precise estimates of value added for these two groups. In general terms, this approach follows that of other CSO and KRSO firm surveys. These surveys are not designed to ensure a high level of precision or accuracy (that is, a small margin of error) for each stratum. Given the number of strata, such a sample would be prohibitively large. Instead, there as here, the objective was to ensure precision in the aggregate. In the present case, this means precision for the estimates of value added for the transportation/storage and other services separately.[1]

To determine the necessary sample size to achieve a desired level of precision, it was necessary to have an idea of the mean and variance of the variable to be estimated. Although this was not available for the services sector (or for transportation and storage), we used findings from the KRSO's survey of internal trade, which should be generally comparable. The mean and standard deviation for monthly revenues in that sample were 21,860 and 99,614 ID, respectively; for value added they were 3,198 and 11,014.[2] These figures suggest a very high variance relative to the mean, as we might expect for a sector that contains a heterogeneous group of enterprises.

Calculations of statistical power incorporated both the expected mean and standard deviation of the variable of interest (we used value added), as well as the stratification of the sample. The calculations also assumed a nonresponse rate of 5 percent. Based on these assumptions, to obtain an estimate with a margin of error of plus or minus 5 percent of the standard deviation of value added,[3] the number of firms in the sample for each survey was estimated to be about 1,620.[4] For the other services group, we also set a minimum of ten enterprises per activity per governorate (that is, per stratum), though in the actual drawing of the sample this minimum was met for all strata. Table F.1 shows the numbers of enterprises in the sample by governorate and activity.

---

[1] While this sample size does not permit statistical precision at the level of each stratum, the stratification still helps to ensure that the sample is representative.

[2] The survey collected data on a monthly basis; the means reported here are the averages of the monthly means.

[3] Meaning that there is a 95 percent probability that the actual mean of value added is no more than 5 percent of a standard deviation of value added above or below the estimated mean value added. More typically, margin of error refers to a range defined as a percentage of the mean of the variable, not its standard deviation. However, given the very high variance of the estimated value added from the trade survey data we are using (which was likely also to be found with other services), achieving a 5 percent margin of error defined this way would imply a prohibitively large sample. Defining the precision based on the standard deviation was more feasible in this case. The resulting overall sample size is generally comparable to other enterprise surveys in the KRI.

[4] The sample size for the construction survey described in Chapter Six was determined in the same way based on the trade survey data, so it also has 1,620 enterprises.

Table F.1
Enterprises by Governorate and Activity in Sample for Survey of Miscellaneous Services

Activity	Duhok	Sulaymaniyah	Erbil	Total
Transport	152	86	112	350
Storage	277	600	399	1,276
Information and Communications	13	33	30	76
Financial and Insurance	14	20	16	50
Real Estate	29	60	63	152
Professional, Technical & Scientific	31	92	65	188
Administrative and Support Services	10	31	25	66
Human Health and Social Work	48	110	106	264
Arts and Recreation	34	41	32	107
Other Services	153	316	256	725
Total	761	1,389	1,104	3,254

A concern with using the 2009 firm census as the sampling frame is that, while this is the necessary approach for these varied activities, the listing in this census is now approximately five years old so is out of date. As we noted in the main text of the report, some share of enterprises was no longer operating or had moved. In such cases, survey coordinators selected replacements from the remaining enterprises of the same type in the same area, where possible (though if a new firm of the same type as the old one occupied the same location, that firm was used). A replacement list organized these enterprises by governorate, district, and activity and was randomly sorted within each governorate/district/activity, permitting selection of a replacement of a similar firm in the same general location.

Structure of the Survey Questionnaire

The complete survey instrument for the miscellaneous services sector is presented in Appendix G in the online companion volume to this report. The instrument for transport and storage is the same, other than the addition of questions on vehicles and storage facilities used by the enterprise. The information collected was also consistent with other surveys the KRSO has conducted as well as other enterprise surveys in various countries. In addition to capturing the information needed to calculate value added (revenues, intermediate costs, changes in fixed capital and various sub items in these categories), information was collected on the characteristics of the firm such as duration of operation and the number of paid and unpaid employees. The sections of the questionnaire were:

1. Basic information about the enterprise
2. Expenditures
3. Revenues (income from sales, interest and rent)
4. Taxes and subsidies

5. Assets
6. Inventories
7. Wages and employees
8. Verification.

Information on revenues and expenditures was collected using the previous month as a reference period. This was considered more appropriate than using the previous year, since most of the sampled enterprises were small and informal and unlikely to keep accurate records of longer periods that could be consulted. However, for each question the respondent was given the option to choose another period (a different month, the past 12 months, the calendar year 2013, etc.) if that was more suitable, and the interviewer could note the period on the form. Hence, managers of more formal enterprises could draw on their books to report on 2013 if they chose. To minimize errors due to recall, we decided to use 2013 as the reference year instead of 2012, which is used for the rest of the GRP calculation.

The use of the month reference period does raise concerns about seasonality. Many activities are seasonal in nature, so that the past month's (or any single month's) information may not be representative of the firm's activities over the course of a year. To address this issue, the questionnaire asked which months the enterprise is active, and asked for total revenues for the year 2013, not just for the reference month.

Workshops and Timing of the Survey

A two-day workshop led by RAND was held at the KRSO in the first week of February to present the surveys and discuss the questionnaires and sampling procedures. In addition to KRSO staff from the central office, two senior survey staff persons from each of the three governorate offices attended. The discussion in the workshop led to adjustment in the questionnaires and helped the planning for the fieldwork.

Training of survey teams began in May 2014. Due to conditions on the ground during the summer of 2014, data collection was delayed, but completed, and survey results were received in August 2014.

Abbreviations

CPI	consumer price index
CSO	Central Statistical Organisation
FISIM	financial intermediation services indirectly measured
GDP	gross domestic product
GRP	gross regional product
ID	Iraqi dinars
IHSES	Iraq Household Socio-Economic Survey
ISIC	International Standard Industrial Classification of All Economic Activities
KIBID	Kurdistan Investment Bank
KRG	Kurdistan Regional Government
KRI	Kurdistan Region—Iraq
KRSO	Kurdistan Regional Statistics Office
MoA	Ministry of Agriculture
MoE	Ministry of Electricity
USD	U.S. dollars

References

Abramzon, Shmuel, Nicholas Burger, Bonnie Ghosh-Dastidar, Peter Glick, Krishna B. Kumar, Francisco Perez-Arce, and Alexandria Smith, *Capacity Building at the Kurdistan Region Statistics Office Through Data Collection*, Santa Monica, Calif.: RAND Corporation, RR-293-KRG, 2014. As of February 9, 2016: http://www.rand.org/pubs/research_reports/RR293.html

Anthony, C. Ross, Louay Constant, Shelly Culbertson, Peter Glick, Krishna B. Kumar, Robin C. Meili, Melinda Moore, Howard J. Shatz, and Georges Vernez, *Making an Impact in the Kurdistan Region—Iraq: Summary of Four Studies to Assess the Present and Future Labor Market, Improve Technical Vocational Education and Training, Reform the Health Sector, and Build Data Collection Capacity*, Santa Monica, Calif.: RAND Corporation, RR-873-KRG, 2015. As of February 9, 2016: http://www.rand.org/pubs/research_reports/RR873.html

Asiacell Communications PJSC–Sulaymaniyah, *Final Accounts Report for the Year Ended on December 31, 2012*, 2013.

Central Bank of Iraq, website, no date. As of January 7, 2016: http://www.cbi.iq/

Central Statistical Organisation, "National Income," no date. As of January 7, 2016: http://cosit.gov.iq/en/national-accounts-statistics/national-income-reports

———, *Survey Results, Mining and Quarrying for Private Sector, 2009*, 2010.

———, *Report on Private Sector Large Industrial Firms in the Kurdistan Region 2011*, 2012a.

———, *Report on Private Sector Medium Industrial Firms in the Kurdistan Region 2011*, 2012b.

———, *Report on Private Sector Small Industrial Firms in the Kurdistan Region 2011*, 2012c.

———, *Public Use Data for (IHSES2) 2012*, 2012d. As of January 26, 2016: http://cosit.gov.iq/en/home/74-english-categaries/others-e/695-puf-4-en

CSO—*See* Central Statistical Organisation.

Food and Agriculture Association of the United Nations, FAOSTAT, 2013. As of January 8, 2016: http://faostat.fao.org/site/613/DesktopDefault.aspx?PageID=613#ancor

Invest in Group, "Plugging In: Telecom and Internet—Kurdistan Region," October 7, 2013. As of January 7, 2016: http://investingroup.org/review/242/plugging-in-telecom-and-internet-kurdistan/

Kurdistan Region—Iraq Ministry of Agriculture, *Winter and Summer Reports on Agriculture Production in the Kurdistan Region 2011*, 2012.

Mayerhauser, Nicole, and Marshall Reinsdorf, "Housing Services in the National Economic Accounts," memo, U.S. Department of Commerce, Bureau of Economic Analysis, September 11, 2007.

National Council of Applied Economic Research, *Economic Impact Study of Delhi Airport*, 2012.

Statistics New Zealand, "Regional GDP Concepts, Sources and Methods," April 2007.

System of National Accounts 1993, prepared under the auspices of the Inter-Secretariat Working Group on National Accounts, Commission of the European Communities: Eurostat, International Monetary Fund, Organisation for Economic Co-operation and Development, United Nations, and World Bank, 1994. As of January 7, 2016:
http://unstats.un.org/unsd/nationalaccount/docs/1993sna.pdf

System of National Accounts 2008, European Commission, International Monetary Fund, Organisation for Economic Co-operation and Development, United Nations, and World Bank, 2009.

United Nations, Department of Economic and Social Affairs, Statistics Division, *International Recommendations for Distributive Trade Statistics 2008*, Series M, No. 89, 2008a.

———, *International Recommendations for Industrial Statistics 2008*, Series M, No. 90, 2008b.

———, *International Standard Industrial Classification of All Economic Activities, Revision 4*, 2008c.

U.S. Department of Commerce, Bureau of Economic Analysis, *Concepts and Methods of the U.S. National Income and Product Accounts*, Washington, D.C., 2009.

van Tongeren, Jan W., and Jan Bartlema, "KBSNA 2008 Estimates," presentation, February 6, 2010.

Vu Quang, Viet, "GDP by Production Approach: A General Introduction with Emphasis on an Integrated Economic Data Collection Framework," 2009. As of January 7, 2016:
http://unstats.un.org/unsd/China_UNSD_Project/GDP%20by%20production%20approach.pdf

———, "Gross Regional Product (GRP): An Introduction," background paper, International Workshop, Regional Products and Income Accounts, Beijing, China, March 15–17, 2010. As of January 7, 2016:
http://unstats.un.org/unsd/economic_stat/China/background_paper_on_GRP.pdf

The World Bank, "Manufacturing, Value Added (% of GDP)," 2015. As of January 7, 2016:
http://data.worldbank.org/indicator/NV.IND.MANF.ZS

———, "GDP at Market Prices (current US$)," 2016. As of January 8, 2016:
http://data.worldbank.org/indicator/NY.GDP.MKTP.CD/countries